Justin Cude

A N O T H E R

R U S H E D

M O R N I N G

Poems and Stories

What follows is presented as
a work of fiction

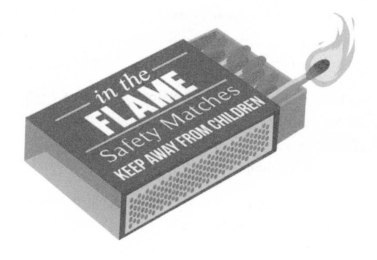

Cover Design and Interior Artwork by Ignacio Andres Paul
Interior Design by Rachael Cox

table of contents

Another restful morning. I do truly
have those. No matter the context of
the morning, I have never enjoyed
being rushed. Try to take it contextually
though even avoiding rushed. Enjoy
it if when wakes up the moment is
infact something at another time you
do enjoy. Slow down. Lit even in the
rushed sense and enjoy, even, if only,
a second of it. Enjoyment is infectious
and can easily be had. You are in
control of this, so control it. It
doesn't take much. Only a little effort
towards moment, and not away
from it.

another rushed morning

i do truly hate those

no matter what the

morning

maybe filled with

i have never enjoyed being rushed

in the

morning

try

to take it though, now

moving forward

enjoy it if

what makes the moment is

something at
another

time

you

do enjoy

slow down a bit

even in the rushed sense

and enjoy

it

even if only

a moment of it

enjoyment is

infectious and

can easily be had

you are in control

of this

so

control it

it doesn't take much

only

a little effort

towards moment

and

not away from it.

her vulnerability

she was beautiful

in

her vulnerability

i had wanted to

see her

in it for the longest

time

it fit her well

like a summers dress and

she wore it

without

shame

more beautiful

now

as woman

then what i had

remembered

of her

as girl

could remind

she was there

standing in it
right

in front of me

but

her vulnerability

it was no longer

mine

she owned

it

now

fully

and with it

she'd

shine.

warm wind left behind from summer

Fall came like it sounds
like a heavy rain
and carried with it images of a different time
same land but
a different
more barren
more familiar terrain.

The leaves changed late last year
and might again before seasons end
I've heard
something from behind the cold took over
warm wind left behind from summer
I suppose
a stranger turned lover, again.

true tonight

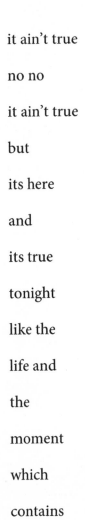

it ain't true

no no

it ain't true

but

its here

and

its true

tonight

like the

life and

the

moment

which

contains

it its

here

and its

true

tonight.

no words, just noise

hammers hammering

car horns blaring ripping

through

a diverse bunch to my

left chattering

cicadas humming a

rapid heart beat

the leaves of the

trees fading with

the wind slabs

of 2x4 of the porch creaking with each

foreign step rumbling

the already loose tables

more voices from over just

down below

on the street

no words, just noise

the sun ablaze scorched

earth and

hazy days all

boiling

pages of my note pad
waving open with a

gust my other

hand now a

paperweight my

writing hand scribbling symbols of

scattered thought

this ones done

no words, just noise.

thunder and lightening in her fists

Don't fall in love with weather patterns, though you will.
This is a seasoned warning yet hard to learn.
They're far too unpredictable.
And they make you feel the same.
And cause damage to the unprepared, though you never can be.
Blue skies don't last for long (but long enough to know them).
I see a storm rolling across the desert.
Thunder and lightening in her fists.
Her lightening burns the sky when you're looking, even if you're not.
And her thunder makes me feel strong again until its gone.

young chinese couple

i sat and i

watched

a young chinese couple

converse

they both

stared out

into the gray sky of

the day

she had a burn

scar on her left forearm and hand

a

purple dress and

read a book more

scars on her knees not

from burn but there

he wore a bohemian necklace and

fanned himself with an oriental

"*shān zi*" glasses as square as

his head and trailed

smoke from his mouth with his

eyes from his

pipe

she was beautiful wonder
if he noticed

she looked at me i

just happen to be looking

too

first

few words back and

forth but

their eyes remained out still

staring never

at one another

always out but

they smiled with their words

as they stared

out

into the gray sky of

the day.

her and the seasons

she

changed

with the seasons

when winter came there she'd

be

warming

my soul but

when the cold would fade

into

the warming sensations of spring the

heat of summer hazy on the

horizon there she'd be

gone again and

there i'd

be

colder than

ever

she

changed

with the seasons and

she liked it that
way

her

way

i'd feel her warmth again and

i knew this and

so did she

and

she

liked it that way

in seasons.

releasing the knot of the yard hose

I'm just no place going nowhere
hidden within sky filled with nothing
but millions of little lights
years away like when you lose your
breath from the impact and stars begin to show the
fight must go on despite the blow and
you finally succumb
allowing your body to do what it does
releasing the knot of the yard hose
realizing the flow of it all and
your movement along with it
the joy it brings just playing in the water.

the fool

I never wanted this. In fact, I thought I was doing everything to avoid it. That's a lie. I never thought there was anything to avoid. I never once thought of this. Never thought it would happen. What a fool. There are occurrences in life, no matter what you do, you just can't avoid them. Somehow, someway, things change. But, I never wanted this. What a fool I was. What a fool I still am. September has come and no word. I disappeared for three days. Took the train from Los Angeles back to New York. I couldn't fly. Too anxious I think. I've had that at times. Scared of it all. I needed to get away, but here I am back in it. It didn't help much either, the trip. A romanticized trek I believed would cleanse me of my fate. Well, I'm still here, in it. Alone along the rustic path back to the city confusion and assumption stampeded my mind, flattening any attempt of mine to just be. To be anything but what I still remain here; alone, afraid, mad at moments, and deeply uncertain of whats to come, or for that matter what has been. I've never been here before. I've had my heart broken, have been down and sad and confused all the same, but never here, not like this. Not this lonely. Never here. The same old now bleaker then before studio apartment, in a dying neighborhood, the one little space that made sense for us, for me for a while, but for us soon enough. I've always enjoyed this little space. It's home, even if only for a short while. It's got all I need. All I thought we would need, even if only for a while. But its different now. It's just a space. A space I can't seem to fill with anything but the emptiness it contains. A space with no peace of mind. One where

17

every desperate thought of mine ricochets off the cold hardened white walls back into my mind. Every cry, scream, every anxious desperation, all the same. Off the wall and back into my mind. A constant concussing of thought, of want, of desire, of longing, and of raw reality, mostly. The frantic rouse of the alarm rings in the morning waking me from nothing, breaking this cycle, even if only for a moment, and I lay there motionless, eyes unable to focus on anything but the crackling paint of the ceiling above, mind unable to calm itself of its relentless desolation. It doesn't stop. It only signals the beginning of another lost day. I've lost many this way, just like this. I've asked the landlord to fix that damn leak. Its from the radiator above. Nothings been done about it. Its been months. Almost a damn year now. A little help is all I ask. From anybody. Work is the same. What work? I've hated it lately. I've battled with it. It's won. I still show up and I still do what's expected, barely, but its not me anymore. I've never done that. I've never wanted to. I'm not the type to just show up, do what's expected, and leave more miserable then I arrived. Lately I have been. Not just with work either. But, with everything. I just show up. Sometimes I don't even do that. Sometimes I just stay behind, locked away from it all. And, if I am there, I'm not really. I'm somewhere else. Somewhere I thought I have been before, but not here. Not this place. Its faceless, without name, no distinct features to attempt to describe it. Its just noise and space. Noise I can't decipher and a space I can't see. But I can hear the noise and I can feel the space, and I know they're real, but I can't tell you how. Either way, I'm still here sort of. Somewhere. But, I'm not really. That's not for me. That's for the dead who still breathe. Breath still creeps in and out of my somber, though. I guess it is me. It has always been, always in there, somewhere, and now its the mask I wear. Unable to tame my internal. Unable to peer out it. Dead, but the breath still moves.

Faint in both depth and drift. This isn't me, but it is now. Every human can be weak, I think. We all are at some points. Hemingway wrote, "The world breaks everyone and afterward many are strong at the broken places." He also wrote, "But those that will not break it kills." Hemingway killed himself. That scares me at times. I've always thought myself to be more a person like him than of another. A person willing to experience and to go searching for the heights and the depths of this life, not wavering from the darkness nor the light that it may provoke. Will provoke I've learned. Facing it and then telling about it. One not allowing the world the pleasure of breaking him. Well, it did. Him and me. Most of us. All of us at times. At least once. The breaking of your whole damn life as you know it. Knew it. I think he had it wrong. It did break him, and then it killed him. What do I know? Nothing as far as I can see. Are you better off accepting the break? Was he unable to accept his? Or was that just a line written because it sounds meaningful and flows with a subtle yet powerful tone, one which fit with the rest of the words before and after. Just a story that tasted right. We've shared similar hobbies even. Boxing and writing and traveling. He drank though. I've stopped that, mostly. Never really was for me, though we all get caught in the pitiful indulgence. We all need something I suppose. We all have something. I'm not Hemingway, but, again, he killed himself, and that scares me sometimes.

What is on musical? Truthfully, at this moment, what is it? Well, there is nothing elaborate, and honestly it feels there is nothing at all. I'm just kind of waiting for my coffee to finish brewing so I can enjoy it and get on with my day ahead. I like this. Make the coffee, Drink the coffee, move on. There's wisdom in this. Something beautiful and simple. I just went back to double over a word I misplaced just a few lines up. 5 lines up to be exact. 5 lines up straight above the second "up" used in this piece. The coffee is close to done. I'll go to it.

thomas

"don't go gentle into that good

night..."

he said

he never finished

what

he wanted to say

in full

but

that's

what

he said

its enough

now

he's dead.

"rage,

rage

against the dying of the light"

he said.

love

love hurts

though i don't

believe

it ever intends

to

love tells

lies

through its

truths.

you can still see them if you look

There are words I write even I don't understand.
Birds way of talking isn't understood either, but I can relate.
I can feel their meaning.
Dog's barks too.
And their occasional whimpers.
The wind speaks too.
With different tones, at different times, for different reasons why.
And, in different seasons.
It even whistles at times.
Misunderstandings are needed for the poetic side of life behind all
the utopian muck being dished out in barrels.
The craters of the moon are beauty marks from a different time.
You can still see them if you look.
An imperfect sphere in a universe constantly changing its mind,
surrounded by a motley bunch of others doing the same.
Cosmic matters though not beyond us.
And the earth is riddled with cancers for us to tell the difference
before its too late.
And I've learned it never is.
Just a trick played to keep you on your toes before stumbling into
quicksand with no trees around.

l.a.d.

a baby cried

a grown man whined

does the noise bother you?

go home

little boy

you can't handle this

brine.

odd

its odd

how you've changed

me

well not just
you

but you and
the

situation

i can smell the

difference i

can taste it

however you can notice
anything

i can notice

it

the difference but

i can't tell you

why

or

how i

can't put words to it
yet

i'll try

but not
yet

more an animal than
ever now

less a human

whatever that means.

there's a hollowness

There's a hollowness we all come to understand at

one point

it can be different for

you and I

its all the same

eventually

but it swallows you

for a time

and it goes unforgotten through your passage

of sensation.

hard to say

you were hard to say that to

thought about it a lot

overthought it

probably

definitely

overthought it

but i said

it and

it

was

hard to say

to you

i regretted it before i even

said it

i regretted it a little

less

once it was off my chest

only for an instant though

but i said it

and

i regretted it

if i found myself

there

in that moment

again

i'd probably

say it

again

and i'd probably

still

feel

this way

but

words don't come back

once said

they linger

or they're filed

but they don't go away

and

they won't come back

and they can ruin

everything of everything

if you're not careful with them.

6:26 pm

and i'm sitting here

writing nothing

just words

trying to make something out
of 'em

its not hard to put

words down

its pretty damn easy actually

if you try

if you have something in that

skull of yours

to say

if you have skin to shed

if there's still blood to let

i'm supposed to meet with people
later

i feel more

at home though

with these words

coming to me

at least they stick around here
longer

at least they're true
maybe.

behind the unknown see'er

I feel as though its not me looking through my own eyes.

I look where something just was and is no longer and feel as if neither am I behind the unknown see'er.

There was life there and now paleness.

Just words I can't touch or see coming to me from nowhere I'm aware of.

Forget about holding them.

They leave too quickly and ink fades when exposed to the light.

The creases of the bedding show signs of life lived, death cheated and laughed at in moans, but I folded half straightening the edges by habit without thinking.

The hair on the bathroom floor, too.

Those are still there.

Somewhere in the air there's a girl now in the jet stream heading in the opposite direction and I hope she's smiling.

I'm picturing her this way.

I was just looking at her and I saw her and now I don't know who's looking.

I don't see anything I'm looking at so it can't be me now, can it?

The white walls do have a texture though.

Wall paper with hints of humanity passed through.

the girl

I met a girl. Who the fuck are you kidding? What I mean is I actually met a person who happens to be of the opposite sex. Not how it sounds, exactly. Only met her, nothing else. Early to the train, I grabbed my seat and began attempting to cozy myself in for the rail ahead. She was late to board. The seat beside me empty. I wished it was hers. It was hers. Thank god. Either her, a girl like her, you, or no one else. Either space for myself or a woman to accompany and to try. Struggling to catch her breath, I heard her shuffling through the isle, having just hurried up the stairs of the cart. Knowing the seat was hers, she claimed it without hesitation and immediately began talking to me the same, without hesitation, as if she knew me. Removing her cardigan, revealing a subtle mist of sweat resting gently against her skin. "A beautiful woman", I thought. Felt rather. Young. Younger than me, but couldn't be by much. And she's still talking to me. Hadn't made eyes yet, but her words and her presence owned the row. They owned me too. I had no option but to become slaved by her being here. I didn't dare talk back, though. I couldn't. I wanted to, but I couldn't. I was blown away and I didn't understand why I was so nervous. But, still below it all I wasn't anywhere near ready. I hadn't been intrigued by another woman in a very long time. I had noticed women over the years but never intrigued like this. I didn't want to. I haven't had to. I was lost in love with another. A love I wanted. A love I thought I'd always know. One I understood and, even within its understanding, longed and strived to understand more. Only weeks ago it was mine. She's

35

only been here less than a minute, anyways. But, she was here and she was talking to me as if she knew me.

"Excuse me, I'm sorry, I'm (the girl). And you?".

"Its ok. No worries. I'm (the boy). Hello." She didn't seem to have any worries in the world. No need for me to imply she had. I was filled with them.

I turn away and glare again out the window at the city we're about to pull away from. Los Angeles at dusk. A burnt place given more life with the shadows. I wanted to, but also didn't want to talk. I just wanted to be, but I also wanted to be more.

"Where are you from?", she continues.

She's from New York. I can tell. Well, and, she just told me without my asking. I could have guessed though, maybe. She has an energy about her only that city can pull out of someone. And, well, that's this trains final stop.

"North Carolina, but I live in Queens now. Almost a year just about."

She was visiting some friends of her's in Los Angeles and was making her way back to the city too, but first was scheduled to stop over in Chicago for a few days before returning. She's a dancer. A singer. Has her own single-person show Off-broadway. A student, though she's considering leaving to focus solely on her art.

"Well, its very nice to meet you (the girl)", removing myself from the conversation early with haste.

"You too, (the boy)," unencumbered.

I wanted to try, just to talk even, but I couldn't. Who knows if she wanted to. I could feel the urge to connect with a woman deep within me, but with my confidence down and my love still maybe intact (you fool), I withdrew. Who am I kidding? I couldn't do it even if I wanted to. And, I didn't really want to. That wasn't even a thought. An innate, highly ephemeral sexual urge, maybe, but not a thought and not a want. I wanted to be back where I was only a few weeks ago. I wanted nothing about this moment. It made me feel worse. "A weak person I am", I thought. You love someone and here you are, a skittish, desperate little boy, wanting to try, not even confident of that, but too frightened and passive to even attempt anyways, and even so the attempt would prove useless and lame. I stood up and made my way to the dining cart as the train slowly pulled away from the station. I looked back. She was leaning over my seat now, smiling through the window with the California sun. No worries in the world. I remained full of them as I stepped through into the next cart. The train crept. I followed.

I will say this: I need to enjoy things more. Don't get me wrong, there are plenty of things I enjoy, things I deeply love to do and to progress with, but what I need and want to be better with is enjoying it all again. I use to do this. It use to come easy. I was intrigued and excited about many things, and my curosity would run wild in the direction of such interest and energy. I want to be out of my head more, and more into the world and all it offers. My goal is to ~~write~~ find the beauty and the energy of each day, and to enjoy it for what it is.

july 14th on a brighter than usual day

time passes slowly

then fades away

dylan said it first

but

i just heard it first

today

i thought something along those

lines

early on this morning looking out

over from a bridge

the past year

it was just

here

i just held it

for a while and

now

its

gone

but

something remains

i just don't see it

yet.

empty space

the door was shut
that day

the old man couldn't
see it

through his eroded vision from

years of looking straight

the father of the young
boy on

the ground

never looked up so

didn't even notice the
door

nor the day

the young boy wondered

what

eyes fixed

on the mystery's behind that
door

leaped

up and opened that

mystery

walked right

through indifferent just

curious to the life

on the other side
an empty room a
lone window

casting

sunlight cutting

through the

emptiness

to the middle of the
room

the young boy began to

play

with nothing but the
space

the father looked up with

foreigner eyes joyed

by the sights and sounds

of his boy

playing

like he once had

in that same room growing

up

the old man's mind

could see for him again

like before time grew him
old

and remembered by sounds

pictures

what that time had provided and

the boy just kept playing

indifferent to

the emptiness

the room

contained

he couldn't see it

though he looked

all around

playing in the empty space

filling an unknown

void

with

life.

when it was good

We slept facing
opposite directions
and spoke with
faraway
hesitations
but,
when it was good...
the sun couldn't shine between us.

We held each other
with cold feet for hours
and forced sweets 'til
they turned sour
but,
when it was good...
the earth never got in the way.

We spit mud
into each others eyes
and pulled wild flowers
knowing they'd die
but,
when it was good....
the wind carried us together.

We wore blinders
to keep from seeing
and threw words like kamikaze knives
despite the bleeding
but,
when it was good...
the rain warmed around us.

those hot louisiana nights

one night

in particular

old red stick

shots rang through

the night

just down below a

gang scatters deeper into

the darkness

you and i

half awake

rolled from my mattress on

the floor to

the floor

unbothered

had a go

no care in the problems of

the world

those hot louisiana nights they

brought the heat.

the window

i looked out

the window

at nothing for my mind

but

kept looking

though

nothing out there

to find

that's mine just

the whole

world,

see.

the black crow we all will meet

The black crow came walking
and approached with small steps.
His wings still work, but
he doesn't have to work that hard if he doesn't want to.
He doesn't stir easy.
But, scares the hell out of you, boy.
I've never seen him fly now that I think about it.
I've seen him walk.
I've seen him watch.
I've seen him cast his wings and cut down through the air like a
Japanese sword
and return to his spot,
without a single flap, but
I've never seen him fly.
A half battered crow,
still the best at what he does.

play with sticks

i use to play with sticks

we all did we'd

be out

all day just

playing with sticks head

home for some dinner

maybe

head back out into the

slowly fading day of

the time

then go

to sleep only to

wake up and do it again

and

that was enough

then

where the fuck have all the sticks
gone?

who's hiding them?

the russian

through the wall

every morning

the old bastard

up early

listening to the same

soviet tunes

from his day

loud and with

conviction

comrade

then

a familiar jazz number

hits

and

the wall

shrinks thinner

then

before

old tricky bastard

touché.

no intermission

The absurdity of sky,
of breath,
the pair,
perpetually held
together
the fact we don't control
either
one can become sick by
the other
can leave us
cannot be felt at times,
or bottled for
emergencies,
yet we need them,
oh how we need them
and yet
we must endure
knowing
they will ever need us
so,
when the wind blows
face it
and
when your breath fills the void
feel it

for there is
no intermission
and
they hold us only a
short while
so,
swim
or
fly within
the nothingness
and
make
something of
it
you coward
to the
stone.

hot coffee

Over the hills of Los Angeles, into the desert of the rail ahead, I sat there staring out of the glass paneled windows of the dining cart, out into the scene of a fading terrain, sipping a bitter coffee made from drip, from an Amtrak styrofoam cup, as the sun turned to nothing and the night blanketed the mood. Panels of glass allowed for an illuminated light, revealing for those looking, the stars above. I was looking. For a moment I felt as if I was off this planet, lost in space, free floating with nothing to grasp onto, nothing holding me down, nothing to keep me here, no air to breath even. Dizzied I reached for the coffee again, but panic struck. I've had these more lately. Even before Spain. The past few months have been coated with an angst over a hidden danger. They started when I was about 15. 14, maybe. They were a lot scarier then. They affected me more. I think because I didn't understand them. Couldn't even talk about them. Didn't know how. Couldn't see their face. The years have brought some understanding but not too much. They still occur, but I can handle them now. Most of them, most of the time. I've learned this to be a relationship more than an attack. A conversation to be a part of rather than to run away from. But, lately, the past few months, they have come back with the same cloaked assault as before, and I'm running. What am I afraid of? What do I fear, now? What is this alarming shock pulsating through me? How do I continue to contain this? Have I contained it? Does it contain me? Will it consume me? Has it already? Maybe I should have just flown home. No, I couldn't. Maybe this is too much isolation. Maybe I'll go crazy, stuck on this train, in my mind, as my directionless over-pouring sorrow drains me of any sense of self and drowns me in my own confused and pathetic loathing. I've always felt a little appreciation for the desert terrain, though. Its life in the midst of death. Land as dry and as dead as the bones we leave behind. Nothing is suppose to survive here, but somehow things do. Nature's redemption. And, the stars are beautiful, aren't they? The heat of the coffee settled me back and the train continued on through the living dead of the time.

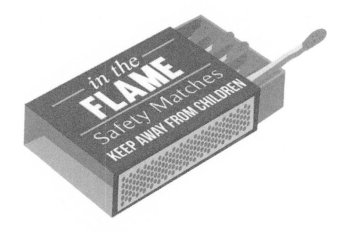

I have not written in a few days. The distraction of having a woman around. Especially one you have feelings for, though I have always felt and expressed some degree of love and affection to any woman I have shared intimate moments with in my life. Not just intimate moments. Interactions with women come with a natural love and affection, and want for that matter. That must be where the distraction stems from. The love. The affection. The want. The want for something. For anything. For any amount and any type of love and affection. We can be such weak animals at times. I have learned this thoroughly over the past few years. Love is the reasoning for this, I have found, as of now. Love for something, Love for anything. It can weaken you in many ways, but your fight for it always remains at least a degree of it

its odd

this feeling

where i'm at

where i seem

to be

one moment

this

the next

very much so

that

how do people

devote

themselves to a state of

being? how

must we keep it

together

through it

all?

how must we

keep

from

seeing?

from

misbelieving? its odd

and its fleeing.

a lone moment

"from the story earlier...

...that was me"

"what?"

nothing a

horribly long moment

of silence

"why didn't you tell
me?"

a look

disbelief uh

oh

"i just did"

another look

shaken

fuck

"no, then...

...why not

then?"

"i don't

know"

the night

the pleasure

the pain

"i'm sorry"

"i just want to lay

here"

"hold me...

...won't you?"

the darkness grows with
understanding

the morning still held us as
the night died

with the

light

two beings

held

alone

together.

i still see you walking in the room

I still see you walking in the room.
Light can be deceiving.
The shadows of a mind unlit by much.
Its hard to see in the dark.
Hard to know what you're feeling.
I smile as the mind adds something that isn't there.
I can see again when it chooses to do that.
But,
I'm blinded by the everyday mosaic.
Patterns aren't easily broken.
But,
when they are you know it.
I still see you walking in the room.
I know it.

in the flame

he came to the

point

where

he chose

the path

which

had

chosen him

he chose the

love

for pain and

turned away from love which
could

have

saved

him

too late and

from what?

most words don't come from

comfort he

learned and

words

his words

at times

were his
only

conversation

time to light the

flame

again for

the pain he

wrote of

a constant ember

but to get it down he'd

have to

walk through the

fire he built

it scared him

at times

collecting scars

but

life ain't meant to be

covered

the burn from

the flame will

die out

use the fuel while

you can

don't waste the pain which

serves

you

coward

die in the flame.

the nothingness

it strangles me at times

the nothingness

sometimes the wind is

able to tame it to

release it

even

to let me know

its

there

but

the mind doesn't

believe

it at times

choosing to focus on
the

sensation-less

moment

which

sparks

it

i'll run to stir my own wind

i'll look to the leaves of the
trees to catch sight of it

i'll blow air from my lungs to the
backs of my hands to

feel it

and

i will

but

it strangles me at times

the nothingness

the trick

the mind

conceives.

as you find the less you know

the mind forgets so easily these days
its wants not its worries

i dream of the world but i'm handed my soul
marred and filled with stories

the sun provides light to tell the difference
wide spaces seem so empty to me

i've cried at the base of a mythical mountain
for my mind "just let it be"

a chinese finger trap holds it now
and only its maker knows it so

few words from the wise have endured the journey
as you find the less you know.

this sweet light

what's wrong

and

whats

right?

i don't

know and

i'm tired of

guessing

live your life

stop with the

harassment the

torment the

wasting away the

thinking

overthinking the

untruthful lame attempts

"go all the way"

he said

"go all the way"

and

live your life

before the

breaking of the

day the

loss of this sweet light.

love fully

love

fully

love below this

its useless

we've all tasted it

its bitterness

it fills the need

for a while

not for very long

love

g-ddamnit

love

not the

falsified

calcified

mummified

crucified

skin of your teeth
sort'a way

no need attempt to describe it

love

g-ddamnit

love.

if the fates allow

I am still
here,
so,
one final effort
before the sun sets
if, of course,
the fates
they do allow.

listening

A friend and I shared a few cigarettes the other day looking out into the Pacific ocean as the sun crept down behind a waveless scape. San Diego sunsets are beautiful, but I was too caught in the dark fog of this new world to even notice. I notice now as I think about it. American Spirit browns. An unfiltered cigarette which fit the mood. Burning my eyes and my throat as we shared a few words about life. I tried to talk about this. He tried to listen. He really tried and I appreciated that. But, I couldn't make sense of anything. The words just fumbled out. Some with cries, others with a raging tone. Some attempting to rest assure the "okay-ness" of all this, and failing. But, most with a sorrow I had never known. The sorrow supported all of my other attempts. He gave his advice and I said, "yeah", but I've always hated advice. It's always the same. Even when its coming from a good friend. Even when its from a person who's been around here longer, or a wise stranger, an old author, whomever. It all sounds the same and it all makes everything seem easy. Makes it all seem like everything you're feeling doesn't mean anything, as if you could choose to be out of it. I didn't choose this and no matter how hard I try, I can't remove this. I've always hated advice. Who knows what's best anyway? Most advice comes with its own bias, its own unaware, unconsidered direct, from words unheard and from one's own undeliberate internal of what may sound good right now, of what may seem as if they know where you're trapped, and the how-to to get out. Advice is narcissistic. It's ignorant. It can be. Silence is beautiful. Listening even more so. Just to hear someone, just to be there with them. Just to listen. To truly tune-in and shut out. Just, even if only, for a moment. He's always been a good friend though, and I don't feel this towards him, but I've always hated advice. He was there, though, and I liked him being so. He did listen and he is my friend and he was just trying to fill the void I was revealing. I don't always feel this way. Its just where I have found myself more times than not lately, finding the darkness of everything rather than the light. The smoke disappeared into a fading wind as the exchange of words followed. We must have smoked the whole pack that night, sitting there, just listening to the crashing of the subtle summer pacific waves, playing a little Dylan on the phone and respecting the silence of one another. Then we got up and left, after the words had left us, and the moment was over. I hope he knows I appreciated him being there. The whole trip. I couldn't have been alone then, and I'm glad I wasn't. He's always been a good friend. He's always been there, and he's always listened.

These past two days I have felt an
intense depression and fatigue, that I have
known before but one that has affected
me heavily in the last 48 hours. I don't
feel good. Sleep has not come easy.
The mornings have both felt as if
sleep hadn't come at all. I've been
scared again of the future. There are a lot
of changes in the horizon and time
seems to be hanging by. Where is my
heart in all this? Where does it
want to be? Where do I intervene and
support or deny? Where am I right now?
With all this? With myself? Again,
is love about now or is it about tomorrow?
Is it immediate or does it exist in the
distal?

g train

late into the early
morning

hours

the damn thing

empty

mostly

just a middling aged
plump latin couple

sitting

thigh to thigh to thigh

me

myself

and i

late into the early
morning

hours

roaring by

stops not

needed at the

time the

next one

doesn't matter the

stop

a raggedy

worn out

young

desperate

lone

bastard

joins the party

late into the early
morning

hours

he's pinned himself

up against the

lifeless

skidding

steel

eyes wandering like

pinballs a

mangled dog

mange'd

ribs flared

skin taut

soon to puncture

hidden beneath an

oversized trench

coat

coated in

blood and

soot and

failed attempts and

mud

blackened by hate and

helpless seconds turned to
years

late into the early
morning

hours

"can i have some

money?"

they look away they

ignore him

another failed attempt

"can i have some

money
man?"

I acknowledge

him

but

say "no" and

"i'm sorry

brother"

eyes still on him

eyes still on me

he backs away further

defeated

only a few small steps further

into the

quicksand

late into the early
morning

hours

he stood there in
stoned

silence

a few lengthened moments then

yells with pain from
hell

"i just want some
help"

then louder again in
breaking

"i just want
help"

then again louder with
fury

"I NEED
HELP"

an ice pick

about 8 inches long with

an old cork shaped
wooden handle

slides between his middle and
ring finger of

his right hand from

beneath the

arm of his oversized

trench coat

his grip squeezing the sap from
the wood

his desperation the marrow from
his bones

the air from
his lungs

the human from
his being

an animal with a
weapon

a monkey with a
jagged bone

a rabid dog with a
meaner temper

a human disconnected
from it all

and lone

the cart continues to

roar

through the cold earth

late into the early
morning

hours

then stops

it doesn't matter which

stop

he tucks the ice pick

back under his big

sleeve

he readies

the doors open

he

leaves

late into the early
morning

hours

the latin couple
they gasp

i
breath

the raggedy

worn out

young

desperate

lone

bastard still

holds his breath

late into the early
morning

hours

next stop mine

i leave

wondering the
difference

him and i
and you

lost within the
rot

of this fall'ing tree

late into the early
morning

hours.

any diner

he'd pick me up

wherever i

was coming from

i'd always seemed to

land late

but

he'd be

there

and

we'd go straight to a diner

any diner

we had a few favorites

all opened

all day

24 hours

7 days

a week

but

we'd go and

we'd sit and

we'd eat and drink coffee and

we'd talk

and

i'll always

love that

we did that.

train through mainland china I

I'm on a train, traveling through mainland China, enroute to a new city, a new experience. At this very moment, I am leaning against a cushioned human shelf up against the window, among a chattering crowd in the dining cart section, a small elevated table in front of me where my keyboard now rests as I bug it with type. To my right, the kitchen dishing out a foreign menu, both by flavor and script; I'm hungry, so I'll try it. "Ni hao. Menu?!" "Ah, xièxie!" To my left, the crowd, filled with wide smiling faces, made up of families, friends, associates and strangers, I'm guessing, and a little girl barfing into a plastic bag, being helped by her un-phased, "been-here-before", loving parents; no one minds, they are busy enjoying the scene, though a few pair of curious eyes are caught by the bald "Meiguórén" (American) lone and curious himself in the corner. I return to my seat, only a short time later to again return back to the dining cart, due mainly to restlessness, part also out of angst; I've never been one to rest easy during travel. I'm too curious. I'm too wound up. I have too much on the mind. I wonder where everyone is heading? And if they're heading there, where ever there is, by choice or by have to? I'm heading now by choice, on return by have to. No one from the looks of it seems concerned, at least on the outside. What about the inside? There are a few dull expressions filling this cart now, whether by idleness, worry, contemplation, or something else of this sort, as we maintain impressive speed, hurling with grace and subtle rocking through farming lands along the route. The younger crowd is still playing. Some drawing, some eating or attempting to eat, others yanking the fake flowers out of their waterless wicker vases placed on each table and examining them, then quickly reaching to yank out another. There's another little girl twirling about, table to table as she ignores the call of I'm guessing her father. She might need to throw up too later on due to the dizziness she's playfully tumbling into. She's having fun though. All the younger crowd is. I don't know about the more-aged crowd anymore. Some are eating or attempting to eat, others are poking around on their phones or laptops, one man is putting pen to paper, maybe he's drawing, and some are examining the fake flowers shoved into their waterless wicker vases, not yanking them out, though. They'd probably like to yank them out. They seem preoccupied this time, though. Aren't we all? I wonder if by choice or by have to? Either way, we're all heading there; somewhere.

a light illuminates until it doesn't

A conversation about race
spotlights in the forefront while a fan
wobbles above at an ineffective rate.
There's a dog curious'ing around
between the isles of the shadowy cave
filled with silhouettes of wanders from
distant lands, and their words, calling it
home for now.
Poutine minds drench the place in
bitter gravy and provide nothing but
sloppy noise for an overflowing bucket of same'ness.
And,
I sit here,
my drink sweating,
waiting for a bowl of brown sugar.
The door opens.
A light illuminates until it doesn't.
Call it 'night for now.

poetry

is a moment of
truth

you sit down and you watch

you observe

you listen

you feel and

you

write

only of that

moment because

soon it will be

gone

into

another

so

catch it

you won't

see it again

like this.

it was a sunny day

an old man approached
me

said

"life is about keeping

moving

with a straight

forward

attitude"

he was walking
backwards

seemed a bit
paranoid

eyes rolling to the back of
his head

but

it was a sunny day

and i

liked what he said.

there's more in the sky

People want to look
up
and
they are
in vain
and
lavishly

Instead of looking
around
and
joining the
tender
moment
of
humanity
of
earth
of
now

It's easy
to
look
to the
heavens

for
answers

To
castrate
ones
self
from the
nectar
of
common
fortitude

To think there
is
a
hell
before
there is
a
heaven

To think there
is
either

It's easy to
wait
looking
up
in hesitation
for the
skies

to
open

Instead of
serving

Man as
man

Woman as
woman

Us as
us

People as
people

And

Nothing
more

Nothing
less

Than
this

To think we're
saved
without
the
saving

To think we're
damned
because
we
breathe

It's easy to
look
to
the sky
the
background
of
our
illusion

It's hard to
accept
the
illusion
as real
and to
love it
the
more
for it

All it
contains
and
provides

Not
enough
we
cry
falling
victim to
our
pleas

There's more
in
the sky
we
continue to
cry

There's more
in
the sky
we
continue to
lie

There's more
in
the sky
we'll
continue to
try.

p.o.v.

if you give a
man

a

point of
view

you

can change

him

maybe.

just
maybe.

grown too small

a big city
grown to
small

you know

the

streets and

they know

you

too

they

notice your every

move and

you

their's

faces grow familiar

without their

naming and

your

story

is

given not

made

minds of maniacs painting

with a brush they've never

reached for

sight only

tells

so much but

the eyes

believed to

know it all

schizophrenic streets

concrete walls

a big city
grown
too small

or

a narrow mind
grown
too tall

poured rain

from a kettle of

tears

i tricked myself i needed

believin' in

unto a seed

laid and

soiled

blindly

which had fallen out

my pocket

but which i viewed as

the world's

sowing

a narrow mind
grown
too tall.

a cafe called cookies somewhere in thailand

the rain falls
the voices rise
miss you by the stones
whistled to my side
... by a group of obvious nordics, blonde hair and blue eyed.

the food steams
the rain lets
a dog eats some bread
he gets
... its been a while since his last meal, he'd forget.

the day is dark
the clouds they're gray
and I live
to write today
... words provide some light, another way.

the cigarette in chicago

We didn't talk much on the trip, the girl and I. We shared a little of our stories with one another and naturally got to understand a little more about each other, but before any interest from either was shown, outside of my initial desperate, primal infatuation, Chicago was in view. The pass two days were spent mostly walking back and forth from the dining cart to any open seat. The last cart of the train was empty, so I'd spend most my time hidden back there, lying across a row of seats staring out into the blurring scene of desert, then mountains, the grasslands of Kansas and onto the farming fields of Illinois, trying to do anything productive. I was mostly just lost somewhere in between it all; of whats to come and what has been, always leaving the row more confused and sad then before. Tried to teach myself Spanish too but that wasn't coming easy either. A few hours before we had seen a tornado not too far off from the route of the tracks, out my window, and others forming, in the deathly-plain rural land of Illinois. The tornado gave it some life. It was beautiful, kind of, in its own frightening way, much like a woman you know you shouldn't mess with or a door you should never open, but you do. All the passengers were looking upon the ferociousness of nature as it raged closer to the rail. We had no where to go. No left. No right. And trains don't stop on a dime. No reverse. We had to just keep going, full steam ahead (or whatever they run on these days), and hope for the best. I loved this moment. I hadn't felt alive in a few weeks now, and in this moment I felt here. Odd how violence can revive you. Not to anyone or to anything specific. Not limited to one degree of the act. Not saying that I would like to be the one to provide it, either. At times, maybe. But, when violence occurs, and you happen to be near it, life seems to intensify and your entire being becomes shockingly aware, past your own dense numbness. Two others formed. They never touched though. Just two funnels in the air toying with the onlookers worry. The one that did form, it never reached us. It broke apart and the sky cleared. Everything went back to normal. "NEXT STOP, CHICAGO". Chicago was next. With the city in view, and all passengers back in their seats, tidying up their area and getting their things ready, the girl and I shared a few more words which quickly left as the strangers we were just days ago approached again. Her phone rang and she took it. I looked out the window, out into the urban neighborhood we were now slowly steadying through.

"What?!"

"I don't understand!"

"You're a MONSTER! I never want to hear from you again! DON'T EVER CALL ME!"

The girl was crying. I mean horrifically sobbing and covering her trouble which was now buried behind her hands, layered in her lap. I could feel her disbelief and her pain. It was obvious what had just happened. Another broken heart in the long narrative of life and of love. For that moment we shared something, though only one of us knew of this sharing. I wanted to comfort her, but I barely knew her and I didn't know how. I hadn't been comfortable in weeks, and how could I provide any type of comfort for another, anyways. I asked what happened. She couldn't catch her breath between her tears and erratic ventilation. I don't think she heard me either. Stupid and wrong for me to ask anyways. Not my place to probe. She had really been hurt by whoever that was and whatever they had said or done. Just as days before she had started talking to me as if she knew me, she cried in front of me the same; without shame and without hesitation. The whole cart had their eyes on her now, but she had no care. She was hurt and she felt every ounce of what that hurt could provide.

"A beautiful person", I thought to myself again, just as I had days earlier, as I carefully watched her go through it. People who are able to let go and just feel, just express themselves in the moment, they have a power about them that the timid and the rigid will never know. The train had stopped. The others were filing out, all looking back at the crying girl in my row. I couldn't leave. She was still there, hurting and unaware of the trains arrival. I didn't mind. I had no where quick to be. Just a transfer train to catch within the next couple hours. And, it was nice to feel the emotions of another, so close and so strong. I felt with genuine compassion sorry for her, but no one recently had shared this level of emotion in my life, and I felt grateful to experience again another human's unafraid, untamed, unfiltered expression, no matter its selfish reasoning.

"Would you like to share a cigarette?" I muttered with a hopeful tone.

Her eyes scrambled to see who had asked. Unknowing to her I was still there, blocked from reaching the isle and filing out with the others. She came to and noticed we had reached the platform.

"I'm so sorry. I just... well... I just..."

Her words just fumbled. I understood.

"Trust me, there is nothing to worry about. No problem." I attempted to comfort.

"How about a cigarette?"

She studied me over with wet eyes, as if to see if I, or any man at that moment maybe, could be trusted.

"Yeah, ok."

She grabbed her things and we began to make our way out the cart. She didn't say a word so I remained silent as well. Better that way. Just let the silence be. Out the cart on into the corridor leading out into the stations terminal, she slowly urged forward as I carefully followed behind.

Turning quickly.

"(The boy), I'm sorry, I can't do this right now."

"Ok."

"My friends should be here already to pick me up and I really just want to find them."

"I understand."

"Nice to meet you, though."

"It was nice to meet you, too."

"Bye."

"Goodbye."

And that was it. She hurried now up the corridor and out into the busy Chicago streets. Maybe we'd bump into each other again someday back in the city. It doesn't matter anyway whether we do or don't. I had no intent other than to provide a little comfort, maybe. I understood her want to just leave. Didn't take it personal. Would have been nice to share another moment, but they disappear quickly and we get the ones we get. We had our time. I made my way outside into the cool summer air of the Midwest, leaned on the outside wall of the station and watched as the night continued to darken. In the mood for one still, I smoked a cigarette slow as to feel the moment (to be inside time for while). I wondered where love goes as the cigarette burnt quicker then I had hoped.

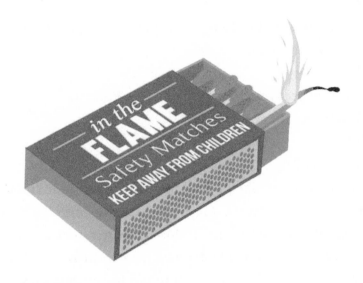

I have not written in this notebook in about 2½, 3 weeks. Crazy how fast the time can go. I just realized, right now, while writing this entry, how important it is to slow down and to think, and to work and to reflect on, this like. Writing helps you to be here. As I write this, I am very conscious of the surrounding world in which I am engulfed, but I am deeply intune and engaged with the movement of this pen and the developing of the mind and thought. This is why you ~~think~~ WRITE. To be here. The past provides the future space to thought, but the here and the now is the action you realize and partake. This is writing. You should always do this. Practice daily. Talk to yourself. Think. Explore. Put words together. Write.

the poison you're sipping

the moment gone
too soon

the past written
in blood

the future an affected butterfly
with scars on its wings

the now too easily blurred
by mud

the mind the cause of it all
but also the cure

the poison you're sipping
you've poured

ain't it fun?

love knocked

i opened

it rang

i answered

it wrote

i replied

it visited

i welcomed

and then it left

why?

love knocked again

i creaked the door

it rang

i let it ring before answering

it wrote

i read it

it visited

we met for coffee

and then it left

and i know why.

but it does

A stale wind has faded, leaving behind it nothing.
The worst sensation is better than that.
A bird crows to no one, flying between trees.
The sun touches everything if you can see it; even if you can't.
A secondhand eye-patch covers my one good eye as the other forgets where its a-looking.
And, words fumble out like contorted Lincoln logs just trying to stand for something.
I just want to believe in something, other than what I'm feeling.
Right or wrong.
Even breath seems fragile when its strong.
And, the mightiest you know will still disappear in seconds.
But, there's a flame which continues to feed it all.
And, our efforts must keep it ablaze.
For, if not, we'd cease far longer than the occasional moment.
Contemplation turned into lost days.
And, nothingness wouldn't seem so bad.
And, color wouldn't seem so beautiful.
And, breath would hold nothing alive.
But it does.

?

what more do you
need?

its there

ready and waiting and

wanting

you

the others appear to be
fading

isn't this what you have always

wanted?

haven't you suffered long

enough

for this

to be?

doesn't this make

you

happy?

what more do you

need?

in the end all will know

i sat down to write today
words of truth from blood

but nothing came too easily
just memories full of mud

they carried with them in their hands
a heaviness full of yearn

then i sat down and cried today
these memories which always burn

and when i try again to say
the words which are so true

i'll do my best to write them down
every line will speak of you

in a world of love and hate
and people who are fighting to prove this wrong

i'll speak of you with truth and pain
to remind only one is strong

and when the words are out and down
they'll speak the truth so real

they'll carry with them a sound so sweet
they'll make one stop to kneel

but when they're read with you in mind
no other trying found

in the end all will know
love is all around.

we all can feel that way

i am truly grateful for

everything

i have a lot of love surrounding me though

at times i act

and speak

as if i am

alone

i am not

we all can feel that way

at times

but

we all have

each other

don't

ever

forget

that

don't suffer alone

its too easy

speak to people and don't be afraid to

be honest with

yourself

and

towards others

have your secrets but

don't make your whole damn life

one

your

everyday

yes

there are truths to be found

within

but there are some also to be found

outside in the

world

from community and

from interaction

don't close yourself

off

in silence

alone all the time.

we all can feel that way.

lately

you've been so
weak

minded

lately so

indecisive and

timid

passive with

your true feelings and

tormented

from within of how to

chose

and

how to

move on

confidently with your

decision

i love you but

i do not like

you of late

others are

affected

by this

just as much as

you

are though

no one truly

knows

where this

infection of them

is coming

from

on

one hand

you know what is wrong and

what is

true for you

and yet

on the other you

have no idea how to

move beyond

this

be bold and

do what your heart

tells you

knowing or not

does not stop

life from happening

or your

ever hurting again.

moon of the morning sky

it's a contradiction
but it happens

it's not supposed to be there
but it is

it's a symbol of the night
but i'm enjoying its

presence

this very morning
amongst a sky bluer than the

richest of ocean

caught within the vastness of life
made visible by the

sun's provide

sketched between the
purest of white wonderful clouds

washed across the

canvas of the scene

my mind grateful for this

all of this

all beyond this even

but

more so for

the accident

grateful for what is

but wasn't meant

to be

for the abstract

nonconformity

of it all

the absurdity

a whole world to be grateful for

beyond this world

even more

but

an accident reminds me

it reminds me of

the mystery which is life

challenges any attempt of mine

to be right

brings to question things i may be

unwilling to confront

to be confronted by

or to completely turn away from

it reminds me its okay

to be

where

you're not suppose to

it can be beautiful even

where am i suppose to be
anyway?

where is the moon suppose to be?

not there
but it is

not here
but i am

and

it's beautiful

all of it

the contradiction

the misplaced

the accident

moon of the morning sky

thank you

deeply

for reminding me.

the first call

You called today. I acted at first as if I was angry. I was but not as great as I had portrayed. Angry just overtook the truth. You told me, plainly, you no longer wanted this. I said things I hadn't meant, but was feeling at the moment. And, that was it. The phone call over. So too our love. To you it was. I felt different and I cried your indifference the rest of the afternoon. The call seemed simple for you. Maybe not. You did take about two months to tell me this. Maybe it wasn't easy. It seemed that way, though. And, after a love we both considered great, a few short moments on the phone belittled every breath we had ever shared. Threw it all away and left me broken hearted. Again, I cried the rest of the afternoon. The season was beginning to cool outside and the heat hadn't yet come on. It was still too early in the season. The building still too old. I sat there, the world muted, and stared at the rack of clothes before me, slid up against the peeling white-painted wall. Things like this don't happen like they do in the movies. A few books have gotten it right. Music is a lie. The popular bullshit at least. A few artists have touched it. I could name them now. You told me what you had to say, and that was it. No sad song playing in the background. No flash between scenes showing your hesitation on the other line, thousands of miles away before doubtfully hanging up the phone on something you might regret. No fading to black to end the story either. No credits to give. No. You said you didn't want this anymore. I acted mad. I wasn't. It was a lie. You said sorry, and goodbye and didn't even wait for me to say mine. I listened to the line cut off. And, that was it. That evening I walked up stairs onto the roof, sat on the railing looking out and cried a little more, then sat in silence and watched as the planes lined in the sky preparing to land into LaGuardia. The world felt empty. I felt alone. The world was still there, but I felt merely an observer to it. An onlooker from another dimension. A ghost, maybe, hidden behind one of those police interrogation mirrors, only I was cemented behind the side looking in and the world didn't even know I was there. They weren't even looking, really. They just saw the mirror and admired themselves in reflection. Someone else walked out onto the roof and didn't even see me. It wasn't that dark yet, and they weren't that far away. They stared out over the railing for a few minutes and walked back inside. Contemplating something within their own life, maybe. Taking a moment to just be. Everything was quiet. I walked inside and cooked a tasteless meal for the night and waited for the phone to ring again. It didn't. Everything remained quiet as I laid there in the dimly lit space and attempted to sleep. I never realized how loud the quiet can be until then. It can be damn deafening. It can keep you up at night. It screams at you, if you let it.

I've been alone most of the day,
and I've enjoyed it. No need to
talk or to entertain. Not that those, a
communicating in general, are bad in any
way, but it is nice to just be sometimes;
to be quiet, alone, yourself, quiet.
I've gotten a decent amount done
as well. Not that productivity or
completing things are always important,
but it does feel good to think
and to do and to plan. I like just
being sometimes. Being an observer
of others and of myself. You
don't always have to be involved.
Its nice to just be. Today, alone, I've
read, I've planned, I've thought, I've watched
and listened, and I've written. These are all
usually better alone. You need that time, that
space, to just be, and to do what is best alone
alone. That's a part of life too. Today the was
that.

release your muffled mind

well

here we are again

another time a

faraway place

both made

familiar by

the path

stumbled

distance is a

lie

time tells its

stories

too

i've learned

only one truth though i

can't remember it

better that way

anyway

time has told me many

stories

none seem to

stick

distance has come

between

but you're

never that far

away

nothing to be that far

away

from

anyhow

there's

nothing to hide from there's

nowhere to hide

nothing to run from and

you'll grow tired if you

try

looking too long for the

sun has

blinded me before but

so too has staring at the

ground

moments turned to

irreversible surgeries you're
known by

well

here we are

another place a

time

faraway

from then

don't make it the same

stupid

release your muffled mind

clear the dirt from your lenses

see
g-ddamnit

be.

you can't stop the world

and

you shouldn't try

its not going anywhere

we will soon enough

you and i

either way

the unknown

its there

no worries to that idea

all we know is the world

its all we have

its all we are

don't try to stop the world

you can't

you are the world

don't you know

you're not separate to the whole

it's easy to not believe this

to believe against it even

but

believe it

the air comes from somewhere

so does the light

i didn't build the ground

but i'm on it

i didn't paint the sky

but within it i move

water was here before us

and from it we come

fire is what brought us here

it fuels our way

you can't stop the world

you can't stop it

you can't stop the world

you can't stop it

and

you shouldn't

try.

motion pictures not remembered for very long

I sit in cafes, alone mostly, and watch through a window the scene which changes by the second.

Scooters scooting by, people flashing past, both directions of the 2D panel, lights blurring like the tail of a jet liner in the sky, a reminder of the trail cut through.

Not many animals here, outside of the occasional beasts who stop from the other side to peer in.

An oriental women, girl rather, is combing her hair with clawed fingers.

The waitress is beautiful and I don't think she knows it.

A great universal alignment when you see it.

Her smile, her words, the way she controls the place, her indiscretions, her presence; the way her pants fit.

The wine hasn't seeped into my blood yet.

It's wandering.

The wine will help soon enough.

I want a cigarette.

A good one.

Hand rolled and loose.

The lights of the cafe make me feel a role in a Woody Allen film.

Stuck in time and the ways of then.

The scene through the window still changing.

Motion pictures not remembered for very long.

I see a lot but don't notice much.

Why do we notice what we do?
The wine has crossed the blood-brain barrier.
It begins its work.
I'll order another.
Its quiet in here now.
An early morning before the sun.
Not far from it.
Not too far from anything, though the deserts out there too.
Just beyond the brick.

the cold seemed to hold you tighter

summers seem to be a

thing

of the past

for me

something only felt as
a kid

i'd always seem to be

alone

in the summer or

working some

odd job

on the road or

away

always away

it was like

clockwork

when the summer
came

the colder months always seemed

more

abundant

always had
more

life

to them or

at least for me they
did

more warmth

summers seem to always be so

stale

to me

too ideal

too waited on

too talked about

too believed in

the cold seemed to hold you tighter

though i'd always
enjoyed and

endured

the heat

i could always feel my own
flame

furnace my own
being

while blanketed by the
hardy

embrace of the
cold

"an invincible summer" of

my own within the
dead of winter as

Camus

would put it

and

that made me happy
too.

summers ain't so bad

i guess

as long as you

can feel them

without holding your

breath.

as simple and as true

i miss you and

i love

you

and

thats as

simple

and as

true

as

i can say

it

to

you

anymore.

the journey's longer than i thought

like the sunshine after
the rain

the returning of an oceans' wave after
retreat

the inhale of breath after
exhalation

life is dynamic

love all the more
so

presence with love is vital

but

this is often learned from times of its
absence

no sunrise will ever look the
same

no wave will ever hug the shore as the
one before it

and

no breath will ever bring about the same sensation of life
as its prior

where there once was

there is no more

but it will return

only different then

before.

the only fight worth a damn

numb

yourself to

realize

the

mediocrity

of

everything

and be

ok

with this

feel it

all of it

its too
easy

but

then rip
yourself

away from

its oppressive
clutches

and then

challenge yourself to

never

go

there

again

you must learn

its

stranglehold

first

to fight for the

air of your
life

its too
easy

too loose

its too
easy

to give up

its too

easy

to accept

without

knowing

where it

drags you

fight for the

air of your
life

and

don't ever go there
again

a single taste is

enough.

acknowledge people

acknowledge people

the worst thing a human

can do to

another is to

ignore

them

even the animals
know this

be kind and

welcoming to

the broken

its not who they

are its

where they live for

now

and where they will remain

if we

deny

them a simple

look can be

enough

even a dog's stare
knows this

who knows

if that man wasn't looking for the
rooftop

before your

head nod

brought him back

down

the stairs

instead

who knows if the reach of your
caring

didn't stop their

reaching

of the

gun

drugs

are released with an

embrace

a look even

just eyes

no need for the
needle

invisible

is an evoked feeling not a

cheap

discounted

cloak from a

buffalo trader

going out of

business

to

block the

howling

wind

isolation is a shut door

locked from the

outside

and

we hold the key

somewhere thrown

into

some crap drawer

in

some crap apartment

in

some crap town

all held together
for

some crap life

acknowledge people

and maybe

you'll realize you

needed this too

maybe you'll find

you're the

poor bum

who needs

the saving.

behind that door

there's so many things in my life that repeat.

maybe for yours, the same.

i've been there before.

i've felt that way.

i've seen where this leads.

i've experienced that pain.

maybe for you, the same.

i know what's behind that door, but i keep opening it.

most moments i know i shouldn't. that could be a fool. but it only takes one.

i usually fall for that moment.

no matter how much thought, how much hesitation. i fall for that moment.

i open it again.

sometimes its me knocking on the door. it's not always answered. it's not always ignored, either.

other times i hear the knocking. sometimes i'll answer. other times i wont. i'll ignore it.

but again, it only takes one. one fool. one moment. and, that door's open again.

and, i know what's behind that door, but its open again.

it's not all bad, though. it's not all good, either.

it's not all the same. it's not all different, i'll admit.

the first step back tends to be different. the first gaze makes it all seem foreign.

i think we want it to be. i believe we need it to be.

then, you notice what hasn't changed. not everything does. most of it, yes. but, not everything.

i believe we want it to be. no, i think we need it to be.

it's not about the changes, though. it's not about the things which remain the same, either.

i don't know what its about. i'm tired of guessing. something invites you in, though. it is welcoming.

there is a home to it.

and you fall for it.

maybe home is what its about. at least a sense of it.

a gypsy's mind yearns for that, too.

a traveler's body.

a sailor's devotion.

an artist's attempt.

a carney's hidden sorrow.

a soldier's sacrifice.

all the same. they yearn for that, too.

at least a sense of it.

but, i know what's behind that door, and its open again.

it's not that, though.

it's not that, anymore.

it's not even yesterday, anymore.

not yet tomorrow, but, not even...

this...
... anymore.

this becomes that.

now its not even that, anymore.

i'm not even me, anymore.

not the me from before.

maybe a sense of it.

maybe for you, the same.

maybe a sense of it.

that could be a fool.

so much uncertainty.

but, i know whats behind that door.

that could be a fool, too.
no.

i know whats behind that door.

but, there's those moments again when i don't.

maybe i've forgotten. maybe i've wanted to have forgotten. maybe i honestly don't know anymore. maybe its all a lie. maybe i've lied to myself. been lied to, maybe.

maybe we all have.

maybe we all do.

no.
i know whats behind that door. but, its open again.

but, i'm not asking why no more.

no expectations.

no thought of how come. no wonder of what if.

they come back around, i'll admit.

but, i know them now. i know their presence and i know their stay, and i know neither are very long. not anymore. not as long as before.

i never expected to pass through here again.

i've learned that too; i've learned that to be a fool.

i was just looking for what was looking for me.

no. that's a fool. i was looking for anything.

i never expected to pass through here again, though.
but, here i am.

again.

the first step, different. the first gaze, foreign.
i know what's behind that door. do i, though?

there are similarities, though. and, there are differences, too.

i know what's behind that door, but this one?

i've been there before, but not here.

i've felt that way, but not this.

i've seen where this leads, but not end.

i've experienced that pain, and i will again.

never have i felt like this before, though.

and, never will i again. not exactly like this. no, not ever again.
not exactly like this.

there is no door. the whole damn thing a fool.

there's only this. that from before. and then, maybe, there's more.

we're all exposed to it.

subjected, rather.

behind that door, no longer i hide.

my mind no longer blind.

blocked.

closed.

shut.

that could be fool. it only takes one. remember?
there is no door, though.

there's only this. that from before. and then, maybe, there's more.

behind that door, from my mind, no longer i hide.

the other day on the ledge

The other day on the ledge, looking out into the evening of the awakening city, I sat there, as you all communed just inside through the window, and quietly panicked over nothing. You came outside and tried to console me, but in a way I rejected this. I hate myself for this. I still do to this day. I don't know why it happened, but it did and I can't get that back. You gave me a look of disappointment and went back inside with your friends. I don't blame you. I just sat there, staring out into the orange sky and continued to inwardly panic over nothing, legs stretched out in front of me, my socked-feet flattened against the balcony railing, toes partially wrapped around the ones they touched, arms lengthened to my sides, hands scrapping to clench the slippery terra-cotta colored tile of the balcony floor as if I was attempting to grip the ground as not to fall, or to jump, or to be pulled or pushed away from this ledge of life I was currently lost from. I felt the world could tip over at any moment and with it I'd fall forever towards nothing, constantly fearing something which would never end or come to be, no ground to catch me. I was conscious of my state but not of mine or the worlds reasonings for it. I felt not myself, even less an able or worthy participant for the trip, for the day, for the world, or this moment, and remained there alone until the agitation subsided enough and I stepped through the window back into the room. I grabbed a seat as to join the moment. You sat on my lap and your warmth brought me back.

The day has turned. The morning and early afternoon were beautiful, but the day has turned and with it the smog has rolled in. Odd to think that is such a relatively new phrase for the world's inhabitants to have to use. "The smog has rolled in!" We are some dirty animals at times. I wonder when and if I look back at this journal one day what the world, and the air of the space I am in at the time of that re-reading, will be like. I hope to not be in this air much longer it won't be, this I have decided. This won't last much longer. There has been a lot to be grateful for in the past year and 3 months, but it, I believe, is coming to its natural end. Not an abrupt un-timely ending, but its natural way; the time when all things transition from one thing on into another, when it is suppose to. When it just does.

the mangled cat on the roof

with me

now

trolls

me

in her search for

food

the only

currency

she currently

understands

maybe only

ever

understood

a simple meal in front of
me

soup

salad

bread

i turn to look

shes closer now

thin frame with

thinner skin

wild eyes and

ears and

hair and

stare

in hunt for

survival

i throw a piece

bread

the other way

she follows

frantically and

disappears behind the

ledge

it feels good to help

even if only

for

a mangled cat on the roof.

written words

the words i write i

leave

them i

don't erase

them

because

i

can't

i

can't

change

them

you see.

her feminine ways, they know

The world is speaking to me.
My hearing seems muffled.
I feel her words but don't understand them.
Like a cold wind I feel them.
All concepts have left me.
Feeling is what I need.
These are her words touching me without reason.
There doesn't always have to be.
There isn't now, I believe.
There just is.
Is what happened and is what's happening.
Thinking doesn't help.
There's a place for it, but, not now.
It will only drown you, now.
You can't hold your breath forever.
Your treading will tire.
Or, a wave will pummel you, pulling you under.
Find land.
Feel the earth.
Skin to skin.
Life to source of it.
And, feel what her rawness provides.
Don't be afraid.
She knows and she will.
Her feminine ways, they know.

another lifetime

was it another lifetime

the love we thought we
knew

when innocence fled the
night

and

flesh was what
remained

yeah

we played the game

and

thought we'd won

but

it ain't for the timid

not to say we were

but

we sure did act like it
at times

and

yet

at many others

at most

we simply

and
devoutly

obeyed

the

sensation

no thought

no worry

no

expectation

we obeyed our desire

and

abided by

its offering

its instruction

it's

liberation

what happened?

what things got in

the way?

what allowed them?

memories

when the memories

stop

forming

oh

how easily

those

passed

roam again

as if the

day

had never

turned
to

night

as if the

dial

never
shadowed

the light.

guess i had to be reminded

I strained hard the other day
I caught myself
to piss away
someone else's shit
from the back wall
of a public toilet
after writing a poem
a few lines which
made me feel
more human.

I guess I had
to be reminded.

But, I went back to writing
anyway.

the living

the odd thing about life

or

rather

the living

is

you're already

dead

so

how to live

with

this

knowing?

see.

hear.

smell.

taste.

feel.

be.

changing

doesn't say the world is

collapsing

not bad

not good

not better

nor worse

just

different

where do we

find

the idea

anything is to

remain

forever?

the world says

otherwise

why do we allow

change

control of

our

emotion? why

is it a part of our

innate

to

hold

on? why

is it so

hard to

let go?

the only fight worth a damn
to hands untouched

What strange times we're living in.
The times they have-a done changed, old friend.
Thanks for the poetic warning.
A scene far stranger than the governments anti-psychedelic propaganda campaigns of the sunshine years.
Only the lookers could see this coming.
You can't unsee this madness unfolding.
You don't come back from this trip.
      Neither might the world.
What an abstraction on the horizon.
I've seen light from the cracks once or twice.
Leonard told us to look.
Gold even poured once before.
The mind's alchemy says twice, and might again.
But concrete dries quicker than it mixes, and they mix it quickly these days, don't they?
And, I might be gone a long ole' time.
That's the way its been feeling.
Ghosts from the past made human again.
Sleeping with those still more recent.
Darkness dies to light then has its revenge again before its over.
A worthy opponent who shocks the crowd with each landed blow.
An underdog for unknown reasons with blood in his eyes from years of irreversible attrition.

The only fight worth a damn to hands untouched.
The birds still fly south though we've confused them.
It's harder now to know the way.
I've slept under clear skies with no stars.
But have held the sun in winter til dawn.
The world needs her then so I must stand to go despite the cold.
Wild poppies provide rich and vital blood for the fields they devour.
And color when you chose to look at life for the way she moves.

love and sensation of

I was set to leave early the next morning. We laid there, cramped on the couch of your friends flat, the window open inviting in the endemic aroma and tempting touch of wind only a country as sensual as Spain could conceive and share with all whom it held. The TV was left on from the evening we had spent with your friends watching some stupid rom-com. We must had fallen into sleep long enough for them to wander back into their rooms to do the same, but not long enough for the film to finish. I reached for the remote, attempting to not awaken you. You stirred a bit. I've always enjoyed your way of doing so; never further away, always closer. The TV off now, the light of the city breaking in, a puddle of your saliva collecting on my chest, the sweat building between our entangled limbs, the thought that I'd be gone only a little while from now and how fast that little while always seems to pass, and the taste of regret I contained from the way I was during our time together here. Morning would be here soon. I'd rather be awake to feel this than to sleep alone with my worry. No dream could provide what this simple conscious moment was. Despite my thoughts, and the anxiety which had filled me lately, this moment held within its grasp everything I have or will ever want or need; love and sensation of. Morning had come, and with it melancholy from the time which had fleeted. It was just last night. It was just yesterday. Eyes closed for only a moment, it felt. It was just then, and here we are now. Having stuffed my bag the evening before, before the movie, I sat there and watched as you and a friend prepared for your trip set to leave the same day, only by train, heading south to the sea to a city neither of you had ever been. I asked if you wanted help, but you shrugged it off as if a stranger were asking to dig through your things. I didn't understand this, but I had felt it for the first time between us just days before. Maybe we both had. I had rented a room for a night so we could spend some time together without your knowing, a surprise I wanted it to be, to have alone time we hadn't had during the trip. It was a small, quaint flat on a different part of town, in an old building which provided its character, but decorated with a slight modern touch, but not too much as to destroy its story. We hadn't made love in a few days now, so I thought some time alone, some time to touch and then to relax away from the world for a bit would be fulfilling for us both. I was wrong. It all felt forced. The room, the part of town, the way I surprised you with it, the love we attempted to make, the way we laid there from night until morning. It was forced. I forced it. You can't force these things. You can't force love. You can't force anything you want to grow. We both could tell. We both wore expressions of forlorn which told this. And, I held on to this feeling for way too long. And, here it was again; strangers occupying the same space. I would be in the air soon on a 7 hour flight back west, over that confused ocean. But, I didn't want to leave. I wanted only to rewind the days which had left and do them again. Have a chance to live them differently. Another attempt at where I felt I had neurotically imposed myself, and my inner dealings of the time. Where the time goes when you're lost within yourself.

This morning, at this exact moment in my life, I am deeply grateful for all the love I have known and loved in return. Despite any past, or any future they may live, I am grateful for them, because love is what this life is all about. Simple as that. I am also grateful for this pen and notebook. When I sit or write ~~it with~~ with them they provide me many things; a goal to fill the page, a page with limits and a specific task, time to sit, to think and to finish a task, something to refer back to when needed, wanted, or least expected. But a wonderful and meaningful pastime that I am grateful for. Also, I am grateful for music. I have come across or have been introduced ~~to~~ to some great music lately, have understood their lyrics and story, and have played them over and over again. Music is a wonderful part of life.

going through it

its powerful to

know

we will

go through it

together.

existence

a whole world to be

grateful

for

all this

an entire

existence

i'm a part of

despite my

occasional

opinions.

long years fade swiftly into smoke of a dying candle

Short stories come from long years of living.

I once met a woman who handed me many in a single night.

Some I can still recite with my eyes closed, others have fled for now.

Some maybe have gone forever, but I won't know until the end.

Others have left nothing in my mind.

Maybe they have, I just haven't heard from them yet.

They're in there dormant maybe just waiting to live.

But, I can't wait around for them to reveal to me anything that may or may not help in my own living.

The sun burns out quickly and who knows what year we're in.

Sitting down for a coffee seems like a trip to me.

Its one of the few things that brings it all back, then, with a bang bigger than the big one we believe in, expand outwards towards areas I'm led to explore, to visit.

Love of a good woman, love of a wild one, both in the same, physical exertion, a read which melts your brain, the occasional hand-rolled cigarette, a few whiskeys or wines have done it temporarily, the wind, a few walks in nature have revealed to me something, feeling breath, an animals stare and affection, travel at times when I'm not looking for it to, a written line which stops me, love towards anything when I try, and coffee, black, sometimes with cinnamon or butter.

There are others but I don't want to taint this with lists.

I also don't want to share everything.

A good secret is OK to have long as your soul doesn't burn you.

As long as you're not scarring yourself.

You have you're own things which reveal to you the world you're looking for.

Don't copy others.

Don't blind yourself either from the world which actually exists.

There is truth in both.

The sky remained gray lately, but I'm aware its of our own doing.

The air we breath is poisoned with our filth.

So to the rivers and the bodies they bleed into.

The land as well, but the world fights back.

Its has to.

Its all it knows.

Not in hate but in life and with love to live that life.

But our filth is dumped into our DNA and we've done it.

This is chosen, not fated.

It blocks the sun, too.

At times I can't see mountains only kilometers away.

I'd say miles but those don't work here.

Not everything works everywhere.

Love tries and its damn good at it most of the time, if we allow it to be.

If we allow ourselves to be.

Love does conquer all, but we've made weapons for that at some turning point in our evolution.

What an idea.

At times I can't see my reflection in a window an arms reach away.

But there are those days when the mountains sit with peaceful calm intensity and my reflection shows compassion for the one it reflects.

Those days keep me hopeful.

One day the sky was mahogany brown.

It was an absurd moment to have passed through.

Was if all were drowning in a pond of spoiled red China tea, or mud.

We put it there and now we must wear masks to keep from suffocating.

Quicksand we've submerged ourselves in with small steps towards progress.

An oddity of the modern world.

Something one day they'll hopefully look back on in disbelief like we have so many times looking back at others mistakes from the past.

How right they seemed then.

Its not a mistake when suffering is packaged and labeled for resale in what we call foreign lands.

Its not a mistake when we can see but look away.

Humanity chooses and it tends to be against ourselves, like a mouse going for the cheese.

Maybe our brains are that simple too.

Maybe we can't see the trap we're walking into.

But, art tells us differently.

Art tells us we can see, radically.

So does love.

More so love.

The abstract and the realism.

If love was there we'd choose differently.

Radically differently.

But cheese looks good to a hungry rat.

Art means nothing when our gaze is locked on the outcome.

Neither does love.

But, when the simpleminded have had their hit, and the daze of satisfaction withers, and the cheese is nothing but cheese, where do we find ourselves?

What are we so hungry for?

Do we really know our own answer to this?

Bob Dylan stares at me as I write this telling me with a single look to keep going but only if you have something to say.

He wears a harmonica on his neck which reminds me the beauty of music.

How powerful that beauty can be and how widespread it's embrace.

"Write that way" he says, and I try.

A girl hugs his arm looking for warmth but provides a fire in the snowy streets of Greenwich Village back when the snow use to stick.

Another, he's confident but only in his questioning.

He knows its a joke to play with.

The next, still confident but with sun glasses on inside after recording attempted answers looking into the unknown of his own, which is also ours.

He's talking to me in still pictures but I hear his words clearly.

His words have always whispered to my soul the truths I've needed to hear.

That there aren't any written in blood but blood still flows, so follow it.

Go where your blood boils, or make it boil if you can.

We all know how.

Answer me this; what have we all been deprived of?

And this too; what are we depriving others of?

I'd say love.

Then I'd ask, why does this deprivation continue?

I'd say we allow it to.

We block it or ignore it, we withhold or we fear its life, or turn away when light from beneath horizon starts to illuminate the memories.

Then I'd know the answer to this deprive.

And I'd say love again, but as an action not as a label.

There's little work this morning so I'm looking in.

We all have so much to say but it never comes out exactly right.

I'm trying just to get it out mostly these days.

It doesn't need to be exactly right.

It never is even when you try for it to be.

Even when you struggle for it.

Just getting it out is enough at times.

There's no wind today either.

Here there's either none or there's the type which can blow you over.

At least it tries to.

Inertia will hold you down.

Or keep you falling forever.

The mind can be heavier than those mountains I can't see at times.

It can also be as light as the dust blown in from the desert just over those mountains.

Dust from the Middle East reaches the shores of Brazil I read once.

I'd rather be blown away or challenge the gods head on.

Inertia is only good in meditation.

Even sleep is dynamic.

Dreams get the heart pumping.

Contemplation has blinded me many times.

The mind never stops but you can sit with it and watch it go by.

And when you do watch it go by, when you can glimpse the light through the filth, when you've said what you've had to say, exactly how you wanted to or not, when suffering is accepted and not feared, when the air you breath is just air, the moment just the moment, those mountains just mountains, your reflection just that, when you understand how much we make-up, the malleability of stories, the degradation of self, the empowerment of illusion, the anything of everything, the everything of anything, love is all remains, and love is there if we get out of our own way.

Short stories can all be summed with a shorter one, and can be learned even quicker before those long years fade swiftly into smoke of a dying candle; love.

No story amounts to this, though they're all trying to say it, one way or another.

No words can say it better.

No other action contains more truth, though there are so many which happen.

Everything comes from this, and everything is just attempting to make its way back home to it.

The shortest story in the world makes the most sense, but we write others to hide it, or to attempt to reveal it, to rewrite it to justify our victimhood.

To complicate it.

That's what I just did, and I feel good for relieving myself of the clutter, that is a practice worthwhile, but, yet all this gibberish, all this nonsense, all the these words, one after the other trying to say something, leads back to this; love.

That's it.

That's what we're all really trying to say.

That's what we're all really trying to do.

That's what we all really just need to do.

Just love.

You're allowed to.

something different

though it may be

comfortable

because i

understood it

i was

ready

to understand

something

different.

the more you look into them

good days

and

bad

days

they make up the
bulk

of them

most are nowhere in
between

its easy to think they are

to feel they might
be

to be numbed to they're
reality

but

the more you look into them

the more you

look

you realize

you're either

flying with the
birds

or

drowning with the
world.

i did

both

today.

train through mainland china II

Back in the dining cart again I find myself. It's full this time, again with families and friends, associates and strangers; people. The aroma of the foreign cuisine fills the space as my hunger again toys with the thought of succumbing to its warmth, to its welcome, as others have already decided to do so and have delved in, face first, enjoying the innate pleasantries of its simple yet meaningful serving; there are three plastic microwaveable options to choose from; one with chicken, one with the beef, and the other a vegetable option I believe, but damn do they hit the spot when hunger finds us. A baby awakens and begins to cry, but is quickly eased down by the loving caress of her mothers embrace; she's now sleeping again. Another mother watches as her young boy devours the plastic container of food in front of him; she's concerned and hopeful he finishes it all; you can tell by her look, she's a mother. A dad of two catching some much needed sleep either before the trip begins or now after its end; you can tell by his look; he doesn't have one; eyes closed, body limp, the arm he's slumped upon without doubt asleep as well. Others are still poking away at their phones, maybe texting a loved one, maybe reading an article, perhaps playing some video game, or maybe doing whatever it is that makes them happy; it doesn't matter, let them enjoy it if they do. Some are conversing amongst each other as we continue our trek through this massive stretch of farm land, still hurling by, still subtly rocking; their conversations remaining as foreign to me as the menu, but their presence shares a commonplace; their warmth, their welcome; it doesn't matter what they are talking about, it's human connection and thats a wonderful thing. Another little girl, standing between her fathers legs, head barely clearing the table, appearing to be eating a bowl of noodles for the first time, excessively and forcefully attempting to blow away the heat of the bite, only to find that her efforts are spent having not cooled the spoonful; she's not concerned, shes hungry. She takes a swig of water from a bottle which dwarfs her little hands to wash away the sting of the scalding noodles, coughs because the sip must have gone down the wrong pipe, then hurries back to begin again with another round of excessively and forcefully attempting to blow away the heat of the next scoop; she's enjoying those noodles and she finishes the whole bowl of them in this manner; still unconcerned, tongue slightly burnt, I'm guessing, but fed and happy to be so. Stewardesses carefully toeing around, hurried taking orders and taming the nerves of the crowd as they serve out not only plates and snacks and drink, but more effectively and appealing, attention; they are great at what they do and impressively patient; also, a sight for sore eyes I'm unashamed to admit, or admire. Farm land has turned into outskirts of towns, still rural, but in its own ways charming; I could spend sometime here; only a short while though. And I, the bald lone "Meiguórén", again in the corner, looking around and typing away, taking it all in, and realizing the richness of this amber, of this moment I'm a part of; all of this, and much more my capacity of attention missed, in this one moment, the only one either one of us here can see, but rich enough none the less, no need for anything more. We may be bugs, just stuck in the amber, but this amber is enough. There is everything we could ever need, here, now, in the amber which entraps us.

two mixed together worlds

I was seeking shelter
from what?
I didn't know.
Suddenly a spirit,
it seemed,
approached me
in the strangest of ways,
a stranger
offering a home.
I followed her
to true 18
foreign borders without
western superstitions
bound to cross the line
and conversed about the ways
which brought us here
and how it all
wasn't so bad.
Beautiful even.
We poured our wine
slowly
and we drank it with our words
two mixed
together worlds
for a time
I knew she'd fill my days.

pathetic

sometimes its

ok

to be a pathetic human

being

sometimes you're

lonely

what more excuse do

you

need?

what more

explaining?

don't act so

strong

all the

time

it'll kill you

quicker.

being clear seems a bore

i like deprivation

i like barely being able to

breath

desperation

i've felt clear before

there's nothing
there

and

with it

an emptiness i couldn't
explain

a numbness to the
essential

elements of

life

trial

and overcoming

and failing

and pain

and

mourning

being clear seems a bore

the madness

is where we come from

but clear skies

have
made me smile

before and

could again

i

know they

could.

conversations with a stranger
becoming more familiar

"I woke last night and didn't know where mother had gone."

"Did you find her?"

"It was 3 AM, and the next room has a worse air conditioning."

"Was she there?"

"She was there, but I was worried."

"Why?"

"She doesn't usually do these things. Do you know your blood type?"

"Now that I've been asked, no I don't. I have no idea even. Do you?"

"AB. The mosquitos like this blood. I don't stop getting bitten."

"You've made me want to know my own. I think I should know this information about myself."

"You should get a test. Have you done the test which tells where you're from?"

"I haven't, but I did buy it for someone once. They were 100% of what they are."

"I think I would be, too, though my dad doesn't have a traditional nose or eye brows. We think he is from the west, his family."

"He could be."

"I have to go."

"Good to see you."

"Good see you."

light through the forest

The morning was cold and cloudy like most are in the commencing weeks of fall in the city. Last night and the early morning it provoked unmanned me, and I thought of nothing else as I made my way from the corroding South bond rail, disappearing into the invaded soil and eventually up through Grand Central out into the lingering season, and soul, of my own pair's matching disdain and fate. A beautifully gloom fall New York day. The night had had brought to the surface sensations and an awareness I had been far too long numbed to, unknowingly, and in doing so sent me spiraling towards, well, myself, and my own dwindling understanding of that self. It was ravenous. It was wild. It was both human and animal, the mirror of both. And, it was innately satisfying. But, at the same time, it was inherently removing. It removed me, the entire night, from all that I had fallen into. From the woods I had lost my way in, it had provided a path, or rather a clearing in the highest brush through which the sun was revealed, because, though I could viscerally experience the providing life of the sun, I was still very much so lost within the tangles of the tampering forest. But, and this is the most removed I had ever been, it took me from one experience of love and dropped me unwillingly into the volatile, and untimely, unplanned, unforeseen grasp of another, though I had no interest in being removed, nor thrown, nor clenched in this way. She was honest with me. And I, in return, was honest with her. She told me about once when she had been scared and what she had done in response to that harrowing. I listened, and then I told her what I believed was scaring me, now, and what I thought I was attempting to do to let go of this fear. Though I was honest, I do not believe I was truthful to myself, and in return to her in my sharing. She, I later found, was not truthful in her sharing either, though she was deeply honest, and later truthful in face of her vulnerability which the night had unmasked. We were both vulnerable. We were both bare, emotionally, as unbarred as we had found the night to be. And, we were both willing, though neither of us understood, nor even cared to try, what such willingness would manifest. We parted as quickly as we had met, unknowing if we'd experience one another in person ever again. It didn't matter if we did or didn't, really. I don't mean that in a neglecting way. Just in its Zen-ful truth. We were strangers once and life had endured, and would continue to without. All I wanted was to share a drink, a few trying words, a night, maybe. But here we both were, without thought of how come. How can one do so anyway? Thinking in the face of moments like this ruins those moments and keeps you where you were before the moment ever had the energy to exist. But, we didn't share these thoughts aloud. Maybe in looks, maybe in touch, maybe even in neglect, but not in word. Now, however, I was thinking. And, I bet she was too. Thinking's easy to do when you are alone. It's hard to do when you're tangled with one or surrounded by the crowd. I was lost in thought, now, and with that thought came what usually does when you're searching for what's to come because of something moving. The thinking brain of our species is not solely an advantage. It causes us most of our suffering. It is where suffering manifests, sustains and exists. And, it is at work now, as it will be through it all. Through every waking and sleeping hour. And, pleasure only removes you for so long, before the brush hides again the life of the sun and casts darkness throughout the escape-less labyrinth of the forest, of which we are all lost within. I'm getting ahead of all this. I haven't even left yet. The thinking brain. Fuck. Though the night did provoke an early morning, for us both, we both just laid there in it for a while. I had my arm around her. And, she had her leg and arm around me. A natural position for man and woman after a go. We laid there until the moment came in which it no longer felt right to just lay there in silence. We got up, she got ready in another room, I in the one we had shared, and we met unhurried moments later in the living room of the apartment, where we could see in a different light where the night had turned. Then we laid together again, on the floor, up against the sofa and fell into another silence as the morning continued to awaken, just simply embracing one another. We talked a little about the night and its containing. But, not too much. We didn't waste away with details. We didn't want to ruin or to attempt to explain with words what we had shared, nor what we individually had experienced. A little while longer, moving from the floor on into the kitchen, we attempted to small talk, to bring about some lightness to the moment. She pulled out a little medicine bottle full of marijuana from the fridge. I laughed but told her it wasn't for me anymore, and that I'd better get going. A few silent moments later she was closing the door behind me as I made for the train, southbound back to the city only a few long passing stops away. The morning was cold and cloudy like most are in the commencing weeks of fall in the city. Last night and the early morning it provoked unmanned me, and I thought of nothing else as I walked away from a revealing glimmer of light through the seasons shadowing forest.

I cannot believe that ███ is over. This has been a constant unknowing in my life for the past months, since ███ I did not know what would be once, hence, but here we are and I cannot believe it. I feel good at the moment, at life overall though I still carry with me uncertainties and uneasiness about certain things. I'm happy but they don't disappear because so. I feel humble for reasons, overt but I am aware of why, but I also feel happy for others, those of which I believe I am also aware of why. Love makes less sense to me now than it used to. I would like to understand it more, but I would rather remain unafraid of it than to understand it if one must choose. I have fought to understand it in the past, of late and of old. But, now, I simply went to love, unafraid of its consequences. I have been afraid in love before, it ruins everything.

207

a fool love plays

the last few times we
made

love you

cried

"i'm not

ready

to go"

i didn't want you

to

but i had

said that before

in love

then it

left i

thought i

knew.

what

a fool love

plays.

what

a fool love

comes

to know.

once again

i've been out
there
in the
burning
wind
the ground
roaring
under
and
i've seen
it
and felt
it's
power
it's
rage
til it's
end
and i don't like
new
to
begin
when i can't
see
can't see

back
over
where i've
over where
i've
been
who does?
who can?
who
than?

but i'll turn
either
way
so it goes
now
to the wind
burning
as it does
so it goes
once again

don't you know,
now,
by
now
you're
my
friend, and
always you
always you have

been
and
i'll be there
without,
without
all this,
we'll see,
seen,
seeing,
pretend
and i'll know
you
from back
when?
but we won't feel
like that,
no
not like that, no
not
like that
then
again

so i'll turn now
to the
wind
burning with
and
within,
against
until

faced
with
as it will
we've seen
once again

i won't stop
turning
and the wind
it
wont stop
we learned
burning
and i
won't stop
trying
no,
i can't stop
it's
trying
so i'll keep
turning
and i'll keep
trying
and
i'll

turn now
again
till the
and its

end
to the
still burning
and trying
wind
once again
friend.

they just need a good wind

I am finally starting to find life in others again as I'm loosing it in myself, even if only temporarily.

Their warmth and their laughter, even their doubts, especially their doubts, but, also especially their laughter, show me there exits worlds I don't know but can maybe understand through noticing, by peering behind black clouds which have rolled in with the cold and have in recent past stayed with the hidden thunder of summer, heat lightening shocking the systems without warning or for that matter conclusion.

There are images in the clouds though they mean nothing to a mind stuck inside them, or to a mind which harbors its own late summer, late afternoon southern thunderstorms.

There are great images worth more value just through the clouds but yet still being stuck in the middle blinds a man no matter how poor or broad or precise his vision.

Only wind can disperse storms to nothing, freeing the air for light to show.

Wind can be created from various and highly effective means of motion, all of which we are capable ourselves of producing.

There's hope there if you hear it.

I can flap my wings and though I can't fly like the birds above, I can create motion and I can use my creation to move mountains, though I like where they sit.

Moving clouds will be enough.

They just need a good wind.

what more?

what more is there to
say?

what words are left to
write?

you're born from the
sun

you live with the
day

and you die somewhere into the
night.

i know there are tricks in
between

but

all we can do is
live

try

and love while we
try.

if not

well

why?

nothing more

it isn't lonely

for i have been there before.

its absence

nothing more.

there were four

There were four;

one was a ghost who appeared in memory motels all along the road I held so dear and always would, blanketing me with thoughts of linen and molten blood;

another, a sages' influence without a crown, smiling in search of it in cartwheels listening to its true mothers direct in sun rays from wherever they'd appear, melodies for the mind, shelter from the storm;

the third, and in no particular order anymore, a flash of lightning dancing in a fast moving storm one night across a crumbling desert, mid-year, turned heat lightning over a different terrain for now;

and then, the fourth, a stabled Tennessee Walker from the Far East trotting gracefully in circles emulsifying the hardened earth below with hoofs as soft and as learned as Carolina clouds over freshly churned butter;

but that was then,
and never was,
only a moment thought upon it,
made up
and written
to be read
by no one.

The truth is hard too see.
Even harder to write
or to read even
when you try.

this is life

i'm surrounded by it

a part of it

even

i am life and so is

everything and

everyone

around me

far beyond me,

beyond this place

even more.

yes

this is a moment and

though we are limited in

sight

sometimes

in mind

to our little pipe hole view

of it

this moment is

massive.

it encompasses

everything and

everyone

you know

and don't.

you are only

a part of it

but

you are

very much so

a part

of

it.

this world is

just

people trying

and

animals living

i noticed this

after

spotting

a man struggling to

tie his
shoe

foaming at the mouth

and

a dog shitting on

the
sidewalk

smiling.

this ghost

There's a ghost hanging
around and
whatever sex it is,
whatever animal,
it knows how to
frighten
a man.

The year is unknown but
this ghost has forgotten
time like a shell-shocked
writer telling stories he
can't unsee but
doesn't know how or
why he sees
them and doesn't give
much thought anyway
to either, yet
he keeps telling them in
broken lines.

And this ghost has
a companion
somewhere far
behind tailing
impotently

but with
grit.

And this ghost
doesn't know its
a ghost and
ignores you when
you ask its name
in vain.

And mirrors don't
reflect ghosts only
those things you
actually see.

line of worker ants

My mother came to live with me for a while. I wasn't in a good place and she felt the need to be around. Where I was and what I allowed to consume my mind isolated myself from the world I felt I was no longer in, no longer a part of, and I think she intuitively understood this. A mother's innate. A women's intuition. It can be scary accurate at times. We'd always been able to be honest with one another, and to speak about life unfiltered, without worry of judgement or concern for hurt feelings, though they were from time to time. We never let it stay for too long though. We could speak openly about our worries, our anxieties, our wishes and our disappointments, and because of this, we both gained an understanding of how important a relationship of this making is in life; how honest it allows one to live and how relieving it is to know and to truly feel its existence. She may have taught me this over the years without my knowing. She was always one to say it how she thought it and to do so with emotion, usually at the higher end octaves and the intensity to match. But, always with emotion, and always with love. However, I haven't lived with family in many years now, and was against this at first. I liked my space, and I liked the option to be in it alone if needed or wanted, but she convinced me to be open to it and booked a seat for the next train north before I could argue otherwise. She knew to go ahead and make the decision herself. I don't doubt or question her concern for me in anyway, nor her instinct to care for me, but I do think she also wanted to get away herself, and I love this about her. She's not afraid to just get away at times, to just do what she feels and think nothing of it. She's my mother. I do know her ways a little, and I feel her ways in myself at times. I am a son of hers. Her stay was very much so a normal flow of life. I'd wake in the morning to head out for work, and she'd do the same. She worked from her computer these days, so she could work from anywhere, and brought with her everything she'd need to continue her normal schedule in my apartment. I'd return later in the evening and find her just around. Maybe she had gone shopping that day between her scheduled hours or had just stayed in doors and rested a while, maybe a walk through the neighborhood, or down to Chinatown to try the dim sum she had been bugging about. Nothing about her being there was invasive or burdening in anyway. It was plainly normal. It was just two people intertwining their normal waking lives with one another for a while, and its normalcy provided a great deal of comfort and grounding. A morning came though where I lost it for a moment and I don't know why. She had waken before me. I was rushing around, hurriedly throwing myself and my things together for work when I noticed a line of worker ants orderly single-filing from the kitchen out into the foyer, continuing on under my rack of clothes. I'd be late if I stopped for this so I threw the task hastily to her. She was working at the moment and never liked being bothered when she was busy. She just waved her hands in the air without turning to me as to say, "shut up, I'm working, damnit" (she said damnit a lot when irritated. Never one to really cuss, except for the occasional, always unnatural, F-Bomb), and I just lost it. I felt helpless, wanted to cry but impatiently shouted instead, said things which hurt her and darkened the day for us both and stormed out of the apartment feeling weak and shaken and alone, all over a line of worker ants just laboring away. I know this was wrong but had no idea where it had come from. We had lived in tranquil and understanding terms in

226

the same little studio apartment for a few weeks by that morning, but I lost it. I texted her to say sorry later in the morning. She responded with understanding but said it was probably time for her to leave, to head back home. I told her that wasn't needed, she could stay long as originally planned if she would like, longer even. But, she felt it was time to go and was gone within a few days. She knew it was time to just leave. We made up soon after. We're family. She's my mother and I'm her son and a line of busy worker ants can't break that bond. What a joke. It wasn't the damn ants. It was me. We are such vulnerable animals at times, easily jarred and bothered by the simplest most minuet occurrences of the world. Little ants, doing what their biology instructs them to do, together, as community, bonded by the their common servitude, kept busied by their livings demands, and here I am bothered by this, acting out completely against my own community, as if I am the only one subjected to the common struggles of life or burdened by the demands of our living. I see no lone ant standing away from the line, claiming victim to his existence, his struggle nor his workings. They are all together, doing what it is they are fated to do for survival, tasked with the vocation to live, simply, and to carry on with their communal duty: to live and to die and to work together in between. I haven't been able to do any of these things lately. I haven't been able to remember others during this. This has consumed me. I'm that lone ant, away from the line, who doesn't exist.

Today's very much so feel here and now. I live in some form or way Communautal with those, some of those, who I truly love. There are others obviously who I haven't spoken with today who are no less lost, but nonetheless is Real & Fulfilling and standing to one speak with only one if so So it. The love of just one, & the Connexion and Knowledship, by blood, or not, is enough, and always will be if you allow yourself the vision of Seeing it so. Always see that, never blinding yourself from that truth. But, your ainitialel mission is to love all, not limiting or narrowing your reach. Because, no matter the world love is it.

death the visitor

death

came to me
in

a dream

in form
of

a mist cloud

spit

from the
mouth

of a

snakes
hiss

the tongue
of

a dangerous
woman

her
kiss

the bite
of

Dracula

the grasp
of

a cold
wind

the dogma
of

living

its burden

but

i remained

unconscious
in the
physical

sense

to the

onslaught
of

the energy's
source

it did

nothing

but

frighten

my mind

which is all

there is

the body

is

here

forever

the mind

it

goes

somewhere,

maybe.

it just
did.

hey again heroine

on the roof

one evening past dusk

the night

falling into its sleep

the lights of

the streets

illuminating

strange orange

transparent

cones

to a ground of

grey

i sat there and

smoked a
cigarette

and

watched as the smoke
rolled

slowly into the
nothing

the moon
hidden

behind

poorly
painted

beautiful

messes

the roof
cold and

metallic
and

worn out

brick
and

warped
footing

and

no one

until the scene

changed

like it does

the door flung

open and

two rats walking

on their hind legs

scurried to

the edge
wall

sat down
and

stuck needles in

their arms

from

their hoody
pouches

and

left again

as abruptly as

they had

arrived

still sitting there

looking up with

faraway eyes

into a sky

which

no longer

held them

i stand to
leave

because

i've seen this play
before

too many times
in fact

characters

the same

just different

costumes

laying down the same

lines

following a

script
the mind

of one

of all

adapts to

so many in
fact

i

knew what

was
next

they spot
me

they

panic

because
they think
i

care

they run
and

leave their

droppings

clink-clanking

like a

lost

indian nickel

through a hole in
your

unlucky trousers

and

slam

the door

behind
them

though it

bounced off the

frame

and

opened the

moment
again

i just stood there

still

and

lipped in
mind

whats to come

they never leave

they're con-artists

of a reality

we can't see

a car salesman from
hell

with horrible credit

with snake oil in their
smiles

and

prescription pill
personalities

the fatter rat

with a beard

and a

dumb

backwards
cap

grease on his jeans and

jelly on his
sweater

creeps

towards me with

raccoon
eyes

beady like

BB pellets

shot straight

on a cold day

approaches me

like a hungry whore
who'd

just been fed
but

looking for pity

"hey man..."

"hey again,

heroine..."

"i'm different

this time..."

"i know that look..."

"i've missed you..."

"you don't even

know

who i am..."

"come on man, don't

be like

that..."

"i have nothing to say..."

"i've got
plenty..."

"you've got

nothing

for me..."

"i've got
to

go.

you're

acting
strange.

i'll

see you

around..."

"no you won't..."

he laughs his evil laugh

from something

outside him

and

disappears into the

stale
stair case

of the

pre-war II
building

and

burrows away

from the
world

the other rat

the lanky one

with blonde hair
and

black roots

follows like a

ghost behind

i play some music

burning a candle in
the darkness

for my own

reminder
and

sat there til

i

could feel
again

the smile of a

hopeful man.

if i must

if i must die my own

death

then i must live my own

life

or for what has my breath

been?

and for what has my blood

flowed?

a cigarette stops time

i spot a man

burning a cigarette

in the

smokin' days of

early august and

wonder

does it cool his

mind?

or

does it add to the

flames

of the

time?

he crosses the

street

with a

cool demeanor as

the smoke

traces the

outline

of his

high cheekbones and
tails

frivolously behind

gone

in a

flash

blurred into

sandstorm faces

just a moments

mix with

mine

just a

meaningless

glimpse

of

time

helping

the strangers

mind

with words

he can't

find

today.

endless conversation

sometimes i feel its an

endless conversation

and

you're the only

one

who ever shut

me up

the way i

needed

to be.

just below your belief in horizon

pain narrows
pleasure expands
we're seeking shelter in a foreign land
away
far away
from the visceral
running raw towards everlasting light
which shines on
no one
nowhere
for
no reason
away
from the darkness trying to speak to you
from what you're grappling and losing to disbelieve
from what you won't look at
from what's strangling you with ease
from the returning sun just below your belief in horizon.

what game is this?

what game am i

playing? and,

why don't i seem to

care

who the

loser
is?

what game is

this?

bananas

a failed man

in more ways than

one

might be the

lowest

creature

on
earth

but

throw him a
few

bananas

even if only
one

barely ripe or

slightly bruised

and

he'll be the

proudest
baboon

of the
troop

until he

knows

any better.

like a kiss

in the jungle the other day
i lost my way
searching for something beyond me

"ideas as my maps"
a mind full of traps
i waited for nothing external to guide me

wind now to my back
life having still handing no slack
allowing my breath now to hold me

still lost most the way
but now stealing each day
(like a kiss)
as small skipping stones thrown to, well, throw me.

whatever it may end

there was a life i
wanted

and

i was

tired
of

wanting it

whatever it may
end

up

being i

wanted it .

seeing one another

She and I met a few times more after the night we had shared with each other. I wouldn't call it a relationship, and neither would she I believe if you asked her. I wouldn't call it love, either. And, neither would she if you asked her this too. We'd usually meet somewhere unusual for us both, talk a little bit, touch, kiss, and move on with our lives. A lot of the time spent with each other was in silence, staring into each other's eyes, smiling at moments, sharing concern at others, allowing pieces of our vulnerability in glimpses exchanged during these intense sessions of looking. Riding in the subway cart, standing on the stairs outside the exit of a line, over a meal or a few drinks, up against the side of the nearest building hidden from the street, walking along the harbor, we'd stare at one another and I don't believe either one of us knew exactly why. Not even a hint. Maybe we'd both felt invisible at the time. Maybe we both needed to see and be seen. I couldn't tell you, and again neither could she, I believe, if you asked her now, but the time we had with one another was had, and for reasons we both may never know. Maybe there are no reasons. Maybe we made it this way, allowed it to be this way, maybe, then left it the same just because. Maybe we made it up. She was a lovely person. She'd take photos for fun, but in looking. She had an eye for people, all people, and she would capture their life in still moments she'd stolen from them and provided for others. That was something beautiful about her art. Though it was her eye, it was their live's, even if at only that moment, and she captured it and shared it truthfully, respecting all a part of the exchange in the process. She'd taken a few photos of me the day we had decided to first meet. I always felt unnatural in front of the lens. She'd always have her camera on her and she made you feel seen with her use of it. And, that day, and other moments we shared, she made me feel this way. She made me feel seen. I can't tell you now exactly how or why we decided to stop seeing each other. It just sort of came to its own natural end. Again, it wasn't really a relationship. Not really a love, though there was a strong sense of something. More so a first encounter every time we'd get together. It never felt worn, always new, and I think its best it was kept that way. If I saw her now it would probably feel the same. As if we had known each other before, maybe, but not quite sure. Maybe we'd come across one another before; in the subway maybe, or just outside it, walking down the street, in a cafe, or was it that art show last week? Deep down you'd be certain we had been a part of each others lives before, but we'd never be able to tell when or how or why, so we'd say hello and ask about each others days as if for the first time, again and again and again. That could be called love, but not the one we were both in search for at the time, maybe.

I sit here now, a man who wants only love, and all that comes with that. Most of that I do not understand but I believe it to be our reasoning for being here. Like Bob Dylan said in the opening of his and Scorsese's new documentary, life is not about finding yourself, or anything for that matter. It is about creating yourself, creating things. I don't need to have the love anymore (Because I have). I only need to create it. With myself and with others. I want to stop looking for things, believing in their finding them will be more. I want to create more. I want to create things.

yarn unraveled

a strangers smile

passes

with

no expectations

i'm aware
of

and

i smile

back

without my

own

i'm aware of

time continues

yarn unravels

relief from a

life

bound and
tied

or

the noose

pulled tighter

time continues

yarn

unraveled.

# of a fading season

whimsical women cut through you like wind
from the coastlines of
Barcelona
the end of summer,
again.
the light from their sun burns down to bone
marrow level
they roar with a purr
and
throw thunder at you with their indifferent eyes.
they're all the same,
almost.
made from the same elements the world tries
to hold on to,
from what we try to
strip away,
to hold on to,
and always will,
but never can,
and never will.
and
you can't hold the wind of a fading season
and you may never feel it again.

almost forgotten

i've almost forgotten

what

i so

desperately

had to

say
then

new
words

have

replaced

the
others

though

they stir

up

again

by
senses

burned or
tickled.

reminded of the warmth

reminded of the warmth

the

entanglement i

once loved

to love

to be held by

by choice

but mostly
chance

you don't sweat under blankets

alone

the wind gets in

there's a hole there

now

the sun has left and

winter has arrived but

i'm reminded of the warmth

from

time to
time

despite the

howling

dry wind of

broken truths

of only your own

whispering by
again.

handed a ticket through blood

the circus is in town and i'm handed a ticket through blood.

a strong man melts to nothing at the sight of his sorrow not standing there.

the siamese twins don't share much in common besides loose cloth.

the bearded lady holds on by a thread and smiles through to the strangers.

there are wrestling midgets who don't fit anywhere from what they're told, but they enjoy the company and they let the sweat roll.

the clowns all run around the field playing tricks on each other and you.

and a woman in a box who is soon to be sawed in half by a magician who's lost his touch wonders how she got here.

i hear they have elephants under the tent held together by ego and loose chains, few people in the room for now.

and a lion locked in a cage he can't see with a hurt paw from last weeks show.

the acrobatic brothers don't know each other, and never have and haven't tried and never will.

the cyclops is afraid to lose himself though he dreams as clear as you or i.

and no one likes the room of mirrors, so they reflect nothing in return.

the tunnel of love is a quick ride with a cyclical queue and charges extra for its own separate ticket compared to the other rides despite its tendency to breakdown and rumored to have killed a man before.

there's a fortuneteller wearing bifocals in between the carousel going backwards and a snake tamer who can't find his flute.

and that snake tamer just the night before couldn't sleep because he misses a girl who's never there.

and that snake is in the mood for familiar music and spits poison when he's cranky.

a man who can guess your weight forgets his own with each lame guess.

the $2 kissing booth describes our existence well.

and there's a three legged dog who trails behind the whole gypsy carney from town to town because he's still able to and doesn't have much else to do anyway.

the circus is in town and it may only pass thru once and things pass quicker these days.

and it's just in your backyard.

and you're passed along a ticket, stuffed, unknowingly, into your pocket while standing in line with the others, unaware that any of you had even been in line.

love always

no matter the cost
you

believe it to
take

life without
love

is a complete
waste

a world without
music

without
laughter

without
words and actions

without
art

without
food

without
wind

without anything

without everything

a complete
waste

away

from
ourselves

from
others

from
the light of day and

from
the animals we are by nature

conceived and born and raised and growth
and

death

don't let the world
fool you

don't let the lies we blindly live
rip you

from

this understanding

love always

no matter the cost
we

have learned it to

take.

'johnny got his..."

There are some things you've felt
only you will ever know
Trumbo's
'johnny got his..."
no eyes
no mouth
no nose

limbs blown off, nubs
no touch
no movement
a straightened, hardened spine
castrated
nothing but mind

without context
without clues
without comparison
no similarities
no differences
no nothing
no way to make it known
nothing
outside your dark
and screaming own

then sweat forms, runs
down your brow
the temples of your skull
your eyes burn
your tongue captures the
salt of the earth
rushes where breath still flows
puddles just below and
you find gold
in the struggles of your birth.

no named china poem

a chinese man takes little steps in the

other direction

a chinese work truck pummels over a misplaced speed

bump

a chinese flag, red and yellow with stars contorts itself

in the wind

a chinese taxi screams and whistles then comes to a silent

stop

a chinese cicada sings to no one, goes quiet, then an orchestra erupts

in unison

a chinese cleaning lady, trailed closely by two others of the same
vocation, push bikes and smile with

chatter

a chinese cat rests in the

shade

a chinese bush provides

said shade

a chinese wrestler stretches on small steps and wears a hat to

block the sun

a chinese car is parked lopsided in a crescent

parking lot

a chinese landscaper, with a companion on the job, squat empty handed behind bushes then return to standing height with brush, then adds that brush to a

growing pile

a chinese girl, with a friend, walk towards the sun with their hats down low and their skin covered from

head to toe

and

a foreigner watches all this with nothing of his own

to say today.

decompose

Within my differences
I went walking through the woods
there's a girl there,
half clothed,
dancing with another man
I've long forgotten how to reach
in the moonlight
of an old new-moon
casting enough light to see
but not enough to know the way
so I trip over roots
and fall into ditches covered with dead leaves
which have been slow to
decompose.

more life

nothing you have to

do

but

live

(live live

live

live

live)

that's it

and

write about it if

you

still want to.

you will.

The last page of this journal before I move on to another. There's meaning there, and very relevant in my life at the moment. It's no easy to say the end of one thing and the beginning of another. I may look back at the pages. I won't make it a point to, but I may look back at them one day, and they may make sense to me, or they may not, but either way, the were ~~took~~. Life lived. they actual happen. You don't write them, only after having lived them. So they were real, but they are even now. They have happened. Yes, but they are over now. Move on. You know the consequences of not doing so. Make the next journal just what it will inevitably be; <u>mere life</u>. Nothing you have to do here but live. (Live, live, live, live, live.) That's it. And, write about it you ~~you~~ still want to.

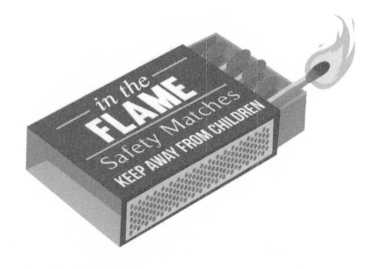

About the Author

JUSTIN CUDE is one of America's best up-and-coming contemporary writers of poetry and prose. He was born in Charlotte, North Carolina, but has since lived around the world in cities including Baton Rouge, San Francisco, New York City and Beijing, China. He published his first collection of poetry and short stories in 2019, 'Another Rushed Morning', when he was twenty-seven. His first published collection of work includes writing full of chaos, trying and awareness. Justin Cude writes realistically about the inherent madness of life and our need to fight for the light just beyond it. His poems and stories deal with writing, death, love and loss, city life and nature, women, the past, the struggle for the present, and our fight for light to see the moment of it all. He has written for online publications such as the DailyStoic.com and is the creator of the CityReadsNYC.com blog. You can follow him on Twitter and Instagram @justcude or subscribe to his writing at JustCude.com or CityReadsNYC.com.

Made in the USA
Las Vegas, NV
23 September 2021